As Steve Jobs once said, "Yuu ___

backward," meaning **we can only know the impact of the things we encounter or learn to the outcomes of our lives by looking back.** Personally, I have had many instances of being completely stumped when faced with choices or difficult work dynamics. It was purely fate that I was given critical pieces of advice that made a huge difference to the ultimate outcome of my career journey. I shudder to imagine the scenario where I didn't receive or take that advice.

For anyone in need of a play book for managing their own success, *Advice to My Younger Self* should be the bible. Jeff offers specific guidance on how to communicate, listen, deal with difficult people and politics, and—importantly—make an impact. The road to success is fraught with challenges, and Jeff illustrates common situations with guidance on how to navigate them. He also points out that it is within everyone's power to find sources of inspiration and support—and this can be the catalyst to achieving greatness. I agree.

SARAH FAY,
Managing Director of Glasswing Ventures

Jeffrey's book is chock full of insightful advice. This leader not only shares from his head but from his heart.

HELENE LERNER,
TV Host and Founder of WomenWorking.com

i

I wish I'd had Jeff's book ten years ago. I would have been a more successful, reflective and balanced leader. Someone who would have been truer to his authentic self. The good news though is that this book isn't just for my younger self. It is for all of us, whether we're starting out or at the pinnacle of our careers. The chapter titles alone could be turned into a poster, and the words in each chapter do justice to those titles. Jeff book is a hitchhiker's guide to developing as a leader, navigating the corporate world, and managing through the post-trust era.

SHIV SINGH,
coauthor of *Savvy: Navigating Fake Companies, Fake Leaders and Fake News in the Post-Trust Era*

Don't let the title fool you. Jeff's words are critical for people well into their careers or just starting out. Too often after the ride starts, people fail to reflect on their journey. Jeff gets it. Seek to understand, embrace discovery, never stop learning, give back, don't fear closing doors, and if you don't like the direction you're headed, choose a new path. This is an easy read and an invaluable reference guide when navigating the twists, turns and potential road blocks in your professional life. It reminds you that no matter what, with proper perspective, you are in control. I'm buying two copies: one for me, and one for my son who is currently a sophomore in college.

DARRYL GEHLY,
Executive Vice President of Skyword

An inspiring and thoughtful collection of anecdotes, wisdom, and recommendations for common roadblocks we all encounter in our working lives. *Advice to My Younger Self* is just as helpful for those looking for career advice as it is for those who manage and mentor others. As the owner of a growing business with a broad team of employees in the creative field, I found Jeff's book to be a valuable reminder that regardless of years of experience, age, or where we are on our career path, the best answers to our questions are often found through the insight of others.

STEVEN RANK,
Founder and Chief Creative Director, SARANKCO:
Creative Studio

I first met Jeff when he was identified to me as a "superstar" by an American Express executive. Jeff is an accomplished leader who has taken his invaluable experience and created an insightful and easy to follow guide with many helpful tools and tips. Whether you are a professional, an entrepreneur, or a young leader, his book is a unique approach to offering people guidance on career decisions and charting a course for learning along the way. Having worked with CEOs and other top talent, I recommend this book to anyone who is interested in professional growth and development. The list he has put together at the end of the book is a real catalyst for thinking about your career more strategically and trusting your intuition.

SANDRA RUPP,
Executive Coach and Anchor, *Career Navigation: 7 Steps to Success*

In the book *Advice to My Younger Self,* Jeff Fleischman unpacks and distills decades of his corporate and personal experiences into a highly readable, relevant, and relatable playbook. Jeff shares his collection of business insights, gleaned from his roles inside some of the world's largest organizations, all using his typical, no-nonsense Brooklyn style. Jeff is an experienced leader, a terrific human being, and *Advice to My Younger Self* is a worthy read.

CHRIS NIELSEN,
Founder of Levatas

ADVICE
TO MY
YOUNGER
SELF

JEFFREY FLEISCHMAN

Hardback: ISBN-13: 978-1-7337242-1-0

Paperback: ISBN-13: 978-1-7337242-3-4

Ebook: ISBN-13: 978-1-7337242-2-7

Library of Congress Cataloging-in-Publication Data

For my family. Then, Now, Forever.

"Keep your face always toward the sunshine—and shadows will fall behind you."

—*Anonymous*

Contents

Foreword

I am always suspicious when someone tells me they want to write a book. Most would-be authors are simply wannabes, people so obsessed with their own perspective that they actually believe they have something to say, and that others want to read it. And then there are those who start the process only to quit once they realize how much effort writing a book requires.

I well know how hard it is to write a book. I wrote my first book as a twenty-six-year-old, fresh out of corporate America and eager to pursue a career as a freelance writer. It was a non-fiction business book that I really had no right nor skill to produce. But a publisher had gotten itself into a jam and contracted with a lawyer with even less skill than I. Desperate, the lawyer turned to me to cowrite it.

I did what every new entrepreneur does: I faked it. I won the contract and then spent the next six months writing and rewriting the book. If you consider that a brain burns about three hundred calories a day, then I burned nearly a million calories to finish that book. I worked six days a week, twelve hours a day. It fulfilled nearly a third of what Malcolm Gladwell claims to be the ten thousand hours needed to master a craft or pursuit. And I walked away convinced I would never write a book again. Too hard. Too time consuming. A pipe dream for most people.

Well, Jeffrey Fleischman isn't most people. When he told me he wanted to write a book, I smiled and just nodded. "That's great," I told him. But in the back of my mind, I knew that less than 1 percent of professionals who say they want to write a book end up actually writing one.

Wow. Jeff did it in spades. Jeff just hasn't written just any book; he's written an incredibly insightful and useful guide that anyone can follow to navigate and manage their career. Distilled from more than 30 years of life in a highly successful career, Jeff has written an easily digestible, imminently followable blueprint that both presents the pitfalls that come with building a career and delivers real-world advice on how to avoid them.

I would disagree with him on just one minor point. *Advice to My Younger Self* isn't meant only for younger people as its name implies. Rather, its advice is useful to anyone at any point in a career.

Jeff lays it all out in workmanlike terms without heavy academic trappings or theoretical ruminations. And it works. From the opening chapter, "Don't Let Anyone Else Define You," Jeff grabbed me. That's because this lesson is one I learned time and again over the course of my own lifetime.

I trace my own path to success back to high school, where my father was the principal. Everyone was quick to define me. I dreaded the first day of school when the teacher read off names. I would wait through the first half of the alphabet until the *M*s, at which time the teacher would call out my last name and an entire classroom would turn to me with the disdain that only the son of the school principal knows.

But what I really love about Jeff's book is that it provides ways to overcome such indignities. How to let go of obsessive thoughts and concerns—those that can hamstring your career—and instead point your attention and energies to more productive tasks.

Jeff takes many of the clichés we have heard about business—such as "Follow Your Passion"—and provides a framework anyone can use to measure their appetite for change, entrepreneurship, or career advancement. He calls it the Want-Competency Matrix, and, had I known about it decades ago, I could have saved a lifetime of angst and anxiety and achieved even more in my career.

So, congratulations, Jeff Fleischman. Not only did you write the book you had promised, but you have written what should be a definitive resource for anyone who wants to jumpstart their career.

Greg Matusky, President at Gregory FCA, Inc.

Introduction

"We know what we are, but know not what we may be."

—*William Shakespeare*

As we get older, we tend to become more introspective about our lives, our careers, the choices we have made or could have made. We often ask ourselves whether we accomplished what we set out to do and whether we are satisfied with our choices. The saying, "I wish I knew then what I know now" has been stuck in my head for a long time. Over a decade ago, I thought about how helpful it would have been to share what I had learned with my younger self. Although they're not an exhaustive list, the chapters in this book were the most relevant topics I wanted to share.

Cognitive development in children entails a progressive learning process, and I believe there is a parallel cognitive development process in our professional lives. Over time, we are shaped by events and interactions with others. We reconcile personal beliefs with contradicting new realities. We learn how to adjust in the future from mistakes made in the past.

Experience is the best teacher; it shapes our thoughts, actions, and opinions. It equips and enables us to be more nimble and proficient as we take on new challenges. Like most of us, I learned much in my career through hands-on experience, as well as from leaders and coworkers. This learning has been continuous, and certain lessons took more time than others for me to fully absorb.

In retrospect, I can see that early in my career, I didn't always have the advice I needed when it would have been most helpful. Career journeys would be far easier if there was a personal coach or Sherpa to guide us at the right places and times. We can't always do it alone. Seeking out guidance and feedback from others is not a sign of weakness; it's a demonstration of maturity.

I created the original *Advice to My Younger Self* list for a single blog post: a summary of the advice and guidance I would have found most valuable in the first decade of my career. I wanted to help others avoid some of the mistakes I've made. I wince thinking about certain situations and how I handled them. Some were unavoidable, and these experiences became great lessons for the future. In other cases, the right guidance would have been invaluable in getting it right the first time.

The original post on LinkedIn, to my surprise, got many more views than I'd expected, and I received notes from people about how useful they found it. The response was serendipitous, and I realized that the list had struck a chord with others. That was the catalyst to write this book. Once I had committed to sharing these insights, the challenge turned to developing the topics. As I began the process, so much came to mind that I was a bit overwhelmed. I created lists and looked for common areas. Eventually I was able to condense the list to the twenty-five areas contained in this book. They cover a wide variety of topics, many of which will likely be relevant at some point in your career.

Most of us go through the same learning curve, which is a combination of experience, coaching, and acquiring new skills. It doesn't matter where you are in your career; the learning never stops. This book is intended as a reference guide—an aid and a catalyst to help you think more deeply and be more introspective about your development.

The following twenty-five chapters consist of experiences, observations, and insights have been invaluable in my development. My hope is that they will resonate and be helpful to you, whether you're first starting out or well into your career.

May this book serve you well on your journey.

"If we don't change the direction we are headed, we will end up where we are going."
—*Chinese Proverb*

---

෨   ෬

Chapter 1

DON'T LET ANYONE ELSE DEFINE WHO YOU ARE.

"Being entirely honest with oneself is a good exercise."
—*Sigmund Freud*

LEADERS COME IN all different styles and personalities. You'll encounter some top-notch managers who provide substantive feedback, help you focus on areas that need refinement, and encourage you to play to your strengths. You'll also work with leaders who readily pigeonhole you into a narrowly defined role, or who apply different standards to you than they do to themselves.

Throughout your career, people will be quick to define what you can or cannot do.

It can be disappointing when you encounter feedback or advice which doesn't line up with your own perceptions of your capabilities, especially when it comes from people you trust or leaders who know a good amount about you. Unfortunately, sometimes others lack sufficient information or context to provide a balanced or helpful perspective.

And when decision makers miss the mark, it can limit or negatively impact the career paths of the people they are trying to help.

Personally, I don't like being told what I can or cannot accomplish. Maybe it's because I'm from Brooklyn, or maybe it's because I'm a perfectionist and criticism flies in the face of being perfect. I honestly believe there isn't anything I couldn't do if I put my mind to it—which of course isn't true. In fact, you can easily convince yourself that you are capable of performing well in any role or position, even if it's a bad fit. I have made this mistake. There were times that I wanted a role or type of position so badly that I convinced myself I could do it. In retrospect, I realized the role was not a good fit.

There will be other times when a leader or others will voice their opinion about what you should do or are capable of doing. At one point, I worked for a senior leader who'd successfully made a significant transition from one functional discipline to another. Granted, he'd had the right skills to succeed, but it was a leap nevertheless. We had a conversation about my desire to make a similar transition, and the essence of his advice was not to do it.

I remember feeling like he for some reason saw himself as being capable of making that kind of change, and yet saw me as incapable of it. In the short term, I was effectively blocked because he wasn't open to my potential. I was disappointed, but I didn't make any rash decisions out of anger or frustration. (Being impulsive in your career decisions may take you from one bad situation into another one.)

Eventually, I was able to move into my desired functional role under a different leader who believed in me and gave me the opportunity.

I excelled in the new role.

At some point in your career, you'll probably be faced with a similar situation. What you want to do may not be what someone else believes you are best suited to do.

Regardless of the circumstances, be wary of rejecting others' opinions outright. Often, a leader gives advice with the best of intentions. Don't refuse to accept feedback unless you are first willing to consider the merits of it. Try to separate out emotions from facts—to be objective in terms of what you truly want to do and what your strengths are.

The first step you should take is to carefully listen to the feedback. The second step is to determine if it's accurate. And the third is to chart a course to move forward.

Step 1: Listen.

1. Is this person genuinely trying to help me?

   Take into account whether the feedback is something they are obligated to provide. Are they simply going through the motions in order to check a box? Or, whether they were obligated or not, did they invest the time to make the feedback relevant and useful?

2. Is the feedback based on facts or on perception and hearsay?

   Does the person giving the feedback provide concrete examples? Or are they speaking in generalities? If the feedback mostly consists of generalizations, ask for specifics. That will help you find out how credible it is.

Step 2: Determine accuracy.

1. Did I expect this feedback, or did it come as a surprise?

    Feedback that comes as a surprise can be a shock, and you may immediately be in denial when you hear it. Give yourself some time to reflect on the feedback. Can you recall instances in which the feedback provided might be valid?

2. Is this feedback consistent with what I hear from others?

    Are there others you can speak with who can substantiate or refute the feedback? If others agree, it's more likely to be credible, and you should find a way to address it.

Step 3: Incorporate the feedback and make changes as needed.

1. Is there a structured plan to address the feedback I received?

    Feedback without an action plan will likely lead to inertia and will not help you to address the areas that were identified. Any development plan should concentrate on addressing focus areas through clear, measurable tasks. If you don't have a development plan, it is your responsibility to create one. Work with your leader or a human resources colleague to structure a plan with specific focus areas and clear metrics to monitor progress. Consider both quantitative and qualitative measurements as appropriate.

2. Is there a plan to revisit my progress in these areas?

    The goal in taking action is to make progress, close gaps, and eliminate blind spots. Continuous feedback can help to ensure that you stay on track. If a plan for revisiting your progress does not exist, create one. If your boss is not engaged, you should seek out another leader willing to help (if possible). Remember to periodically monitor your progress with them.

3. What if the feedback is off the mark?

It can be frustrating if feedback is not accurate. The best option is to use facts to reset a misperception. But even then, you may not change a person's mind.

When it comes time to provide guidance to others, apply the same approach with them that you would want for yourself. Giving advice is one half of a plan, and providing substantive recommendations is the other half.

Even though others will influence and guide you on your journey, you alone will live with the choices you make. Not all your decisions will be perfect. That's okay. Stay focused on your long-term objectives. Remember that your career will have its ups and downs, so be prepared to course correct and stay on track. Don't let anyone else assume that role for you.

And don't ever let anyone else define who you are.

"Your only obligation in any lifetime is to be true to yourself. Being true to anyone else or anything else is... impossible."

—*Richard Bach*

ॐ ॐ

Chapter 2

BE BRAVE AND TRUST YOUR INTUITION.

"Your time is limited, so don't waste it living someone else's life. Don't be trapped by dogma—which is living with the results of other people's thinking. Don't let the noise of others' opinions drown out your own inner voice. And most important, have the courage to follow your heart and intuition."

—Steve Jobs

STEVE JOBS WAS one of the most respected and visionary leaders of his time. He relentlessly pursued his creative vision for how Apple's products should look, feel, and function. He was known for following his intuition… often to the point of being obstinate, inflexible, and unwilling to compromise. Like Steve Jobs, many corporate visionaries have a maniacal focus; they innovate and disrupt in the pursuit of their goals. They are adept at moving quickly, relying on their intuition and leveraging information and people they trust.

In today's fast-paced business climate, decision makers have access to more data than ever before. Yet processing all that data takes time, and agility and speed are crucial to the success of both leaders and companies. Even small delays in progressing forward can put you at a competitive disadvantage.

Your intuition can be your most trusted guide. But I'm not suggesting that you adopt a style that leaves a path of destruction in your wake. Throughout this book, you'll read about the notion of maintaining balance. In this case, it means finding that place between barely scratching the surface and overanalysis when you need to make a decision.

Attaining this balance comes with experience. Having a lack of information or being unable to answer basic questions means that any decision won't be based on a solid foundation. Conversely, overanalysis creates unnecessary delays and increases costs. When the focus is on the analysis rather than making a decision, you're out of balance.

When faced with a decision, take a robust approach to gathering the information you'll need. Make it your practice to take in the perspectives of the people around you, as well as data and any relevant research. Hard facts should be a priority and should always be part of your process. The following framework outlines the core areas in which you should seek out information, as well as questions to consider:

- **People and partners** – Who should you rely on? Can they be objective? What are their motivations? What is their reputation for providing candid, unbiased opinions? What is their track record when it comes to getting the job done?

- **Data and information** – What information do you have? Does it corroborate or contradict a prevailing opinion or company position? Are your sources reliable and trustworthy? Are there gaps in the information that you need to fill in to reach a decision?

- **Determining feasibility** – Do you have all the resources you need to support the decision (staffing, funding)? Have you accounted for the factors that have worked in the past? Are the risks documented and potential impacts understood?

- **Tracking outcomes** – How will you measure success? If the decision involves a new project, what metrics will determine whether you are on track? How will you gather data? How often will you assess the results, and who will you share them with?

In most cases, you will be able to accumulate most of the information you need. But there will be times when circumstances require an immediate (and less informed) decision.

When that happens, trust your intuition. Don't panic, but be prepared for the unexpected. Rely on the information you have and the opinions of people you trust. Understand that things may not go as expected—be prepared to course correct as needed.

There are several impediments that work against expedited decision-making. Table 1 below lists some of the more common situations you're likely to encounter within companies or among leaders. Keep in mind that these scenarios can either be something you face or something you create.

Archetype	Description	Solution
Analysis paralysis	Seemingly endless and redundant analysis causes delays in decision-making and progress.	Define the analyses that are essential to making an informed decision. Avoid superfluous work that will not add value.
Management by committee	Multiple people manage a project with no clear decision maker. This leads to confusion, conflicting decisions, and divergent activities.	Create a RACI (Responsible, Accountable, Consulted, Informed) matrix. This provides team members clearly defined roles and responsibilities. The project leader is accountable for setting up the RACI matrix.
Death by a thousand paper cuts	A multitude of secondary or tertiary activities do not contribute to driving results and outcomes.	Stay focused on core tasks. Emphasis should be placed on those activities that have a clear connection to an outcome.

Archetype	Description	Solution
The meeting after the meeting	Decisions are made and agreed to during planning or team meetings, but some team members undermine those decisions by questioning them in "the meeting after the meeting."	A leader must ensure that team members understand that when a decision is reached, it is final. Fostering a culture in which opinions are valued and encouraged will reduce the potential for second-guessing decisions.
Deer in the headlights	A decision maker has the appropriate information and data yet is reluctant to move forward. This person may be apprehensive about committing to a decision, especially when outcomes are uncertain.	Team members will need to take an assertive approach in getting their leader to make a decision(s). Utilize data and facts to help the leader become comfortable in making a decision. Another tactic is to convey that indecision will have an adverse impact on a desired outcome.

Table 1 – Leadership Archetypes

Learning to use your instincts in conjunction with information and data will empower you to become a more dynamic leader. Over time and with experience, you'll hone the dependability of your gut instinct. Your ability to act quickly and decisively will grow—and with it, your confidence in the decisions you make.

"It is always with excitement that I wake up in the morning wondering what my intuition will toss up to me, like gifts from the sea. I work with it and rely on it. It's my partner."

—*Jonas Salk*

Chapter 3

LISTEN ATTENTIVELY BEFORE SPEAKING; LISTEN WITH THE INTENT TO UNDERSTAND.

"Wisdom is the reward you get for a lifetime of listening when you'd have preferred to talk."

—Doug Larson

I ONCE HAD a leader who made their team feel like they were constantly under a verbal barrage. I eventually became defensive and shut down during meetings and wasn't very motivated. One of my colleagues told me I needed to separate *what* was said from *how* it was said. Although I didn't like the way my leader communicated, I was eventually able to get beyond the tone and focus on the content. Had it not been for that advice, I would have continued to assume the worst and jump to the wrong conclusions because I wasn't listening.

It was an invaluable lesson.

Listening is one of those things we tend to take for granted, but it is an acquired skill. It is a conscious act in which our brains are processing the meanings of words and thoughts, and it takes a concerted effort to become proficient. If there was a single area I needed to focus on early in my career, it was listening. Often I was eager to speak, to be heard, and I focused more on making a point than on listening to what was being said. This sometimes gave the impression that I was unfocused and not on point with my comments. I soon learned that if I did not hone my listening skills, it would hamper my career progression.

Developing good listening skills will take time. Avoid distractions and interruptions, look for nonverbal communications (e.g., expressions, body language), pay attention to tone, and ask probing questions to understand what is being conveyed. Spend less time speaking, and focus on crafting a response to address comments made. Repeat back what you've heard to confirm that your interpretation is on the mark.

Most people assume hearing and listening are the same, but there is a big difference between them. Unless you know the difference, you may never become an effective listener, and this will limit your efficacy as a communicator. Hearing is a physical process of hearing sound; listening is a process of receiving and interpreting what is being said. You may be able to repeat what a person said, but do you understand what they meant? Often people talk past each other because they are advocating a point of view and dig their heels in. Being a selective listener diminishes your ability to understand someone else's point of view. Even though you may not agree with someone, listening makes you more effective in conveying your perspective.

There are many situations in which your ability to listen can make the difference between reaching agreement and hitting an impasse. We all know that emotions sometimes get the best of us. Once a discussion moves beyond logic and reasoning, it can quickly devolve into an emotional tug of war. Stubbornness or unwillingness to listen to someone is usually the culprit in these situations.

Listening is the foundation for strong communication. It will provide a range of benefits throughout your life. These include the ability to gain consensus, resolve conflict, effectively engage others, and improve individual and team performance. Consider the following tactics when mastering the ability to listen:

- **Resolve conflicting points of view:** People don't always agree on priorities or strategic direction, but they can nonetheless come to a meeting of the minds. Try to be objective even when others' views are diametrically opposed to your own. Seek to understand differing points of view and the underlying logic that led others to these perspectives. Focus on facts, not opinions, to reduce the likelihood of devolving into a battle of wills. Frame your responses in ways that are not accusatory or confrontational; base them on specific points expressed by others.

- **Set and align expectations:** Establishing clear expectations upfront will reduce friction and increase the likelihood that people will be aligned. Be explicit about what's expected of all individuals in terms of actions and deliverables. Summarize what was agreed to, and confirm it through email to ensure there is no misinterpretation of what was stated or how you heard it.

- **Align semantics:** There may be times you think you disagree with someone because of how something is expressed, but in reality you're actually in agreement. Seek to understand others' motivations in addition to the words they choose to use. Mimic their logic and body language. By conveying thoughts in their words, you'll accomplish two things: First, you'll get a clearer understanding of their point of view. Second, you'll lower their active resistance to your message, because you're speaking the same language. And that will make them feel more comfortable.

- **Know the right time to engage:** Allow other participants to express their perspectives. In fact, encourage it. Interrupting someone is counterproductive and could derail the conversation. Ask questions to close any gaps in your understanding, and allow others to do the same. Respond to topics as they are raised. When you speak, make sure your communication is clear, concise, and articulates the key points you want to convey.

Communication is a critically important skill, and listening is perhaps its most important component. It will play a vital role throughout your career. If this is an area of weakness for you, don't ignore it. Remember, it is never too late to improve your listening skills. And it becomes increasingly important as you take on more senior roles with greater responsibility. It's incumbent upon a leader to resolve differences before they escalate. Listening is the foundation for making that happen.

Make it a priority to listen with the intent to understand.

"Courage is what it takes to stand up and speak; it's also what it takes to sit down and listen."

—*Anonymous*

ॐ ॐ

Chapter 4

ENSURE YOU HAVE THE FACTS BEFORE TAKING ACTION.

"Get your facts first, and then you can distort 'em as much as you please."

—*Mark Twain,*
as quoted by Rudyard Kipling

A LEADER ONCE told me that a person should believe nothing they hear and 10 percent of what they see. One of the biggest mistakes you can make is to reach a conclusion based on incomplete or inaccurate information. Especially because things are not always what they seem.

Understanding the facts is especially important in situations where agreement and alignment among team members are necessary to move an initiative forward—for instance, in investment prioritization, bidding on work, planning meetings, steering committee meetings, and talent reviews. It is far easier to advocate a position, influence others, or reach a consensus when you have supporting data.

This doesn't run counter to relying on intuition as covered in Chapter 2. Intuition and facts are not mutually exclusive. But intuition or gut feel without facts to support it can sidetrack you. There is a good chance people will not believe you when you simply say, "Trust me on this." Conversely, fact-based decisions devoid of intuition may create their own shortcomings. For example, suppose the facts indicate that you should invest in Product A. However, the new emerging Product B is better, and your gut says over time it will become the top product in its space. The solution should be to focus on Product A but be prepared to shift efforts to Product B when the time is right. Both intuition and facts have a place—knowing how much to rely on each is the challenge.

So how should you navigate situations in which identifying and dealing with facts is critical?

Understand what information is needed and useful. Not every occasion requires an abundance of data. Having too much data can be as bad as having too little. When appropriate, it's advisable to seek out a broad set of sources, each of which can provide a unique perspective. Start by having a game plan to gather a robust set of data, opinions, and research relevant to the situation. Company data should not be your sole source of information. A broad set of sources includes:

- **Internal sources:** company analysis, research, past project performance, strategy and priorities, key stakeholders

- **Competitors:** top competitor strategies, financial performance history, new entrant offerings, product positioning, and sales trends

- **Industry research:** emerging trends in the industry, economic conditions, impact of disruptors, new technology, existing or emerging data capabilities and platforms

- **Consumers:** feedback, preferences, latent wants (what consumers truly need), variations across demographic segments (e.g., age, geography), and buying trends

- **Subject matter experts/influencers:** interviews, research studies, white papers, blog posts, etc.

Once you have the information, synthesize your findings and summarize your conclusions. It is imperative that you establish early on the facts that are agreed to by all parties. This takes the emphasis away from disagreements based on opinions and shifts it to those based on the facts. It is also a solid starting point for discussion, as it enables you to raise questions or challenge priorities without undue influence from emotions. Finally, it is good preparation for the defense of a decision that may face scrutiny from others.

Undisputed facts represent the basis for sound decision-making. When dealing with situations that involve a multitude of opinions, ask questions. Sentiments can vary greatly, and any insight that can substantiate a point of view can be valuable. It's important to separate facts from fiction, especially when the facts run counter to your opinions or those of others.

It is in your best interest to shut down unproductive deliberations. In any company, there will be times when opinions bog down the decision-making process. I call this the taxation of opinion: delays and increased costs created by putting emotions ahead of facts. Thoughts that don't match reality need to be filtered out from further discussion. Be careful, though, to criticize the ideas, not the people who suggest them.

Even when everyone agrees on the facts, sometimes leaders ignore them. They may have differing goals or personal preferences that dictate their priorities. This can lead to poor choices and cause the team or company to fall short of expectations.

Effective leaders, on the other hand, have a keen sense of pulling together and using relevant data to make decisions and set priorities. They recognize that the success of a project or strategy will be highly correlated with its basis in facts. They know it is imperative not to let decisions be tainted by opinions, emotions, or personal preferences.

Corporate cultures also vary when it comes to decision-making. Some will encourage robust discussion and diverse points of view. Others will promote only those ideas and thoughts that can be validated with facts or research. Make sure you understand your company's culture in order to most effectively influence the decision-making process. Once, when I had recently joined a firm, I found myself labeled as an overanalyzer. I'd been taking the same approach I had used for over a decade with a different company. Unfortunately, I hadn't realized my new firm did not advocate the same deep, detailed analysis. It was viewed as unnecessary. Needless to say, I quickly adapted.

Remember that everyone is entitled to their own opinions, but not their own facts. Opinions can be so entrenched that some people will ignore the facts. The best way to respond is to get the facts straight and present them to others. Making informed, data-based decisions is an effective strategy to increase your likelihood of success.

"Facts are stubborn things; and whatever may be our wishes, our inclinations, or the dictates of our passions, they cannot alter the state of facts and evidence."

—John Adams

ॐ ॐ

Chapter 5

ACCEPT CHANGE; IT IS THE ONE CONSTANT THAT WILL ALWAYS EXIST.

"It is not necessary to change. Survival is not mandatory."

—W. Edwards Deming

WE'VE ALL HEARD the sayings "The only thing you can count on is change" and "Change is constant." Jobs are created or phased out, deals won or lost, companies bought or sold. Change cannot be avoided, and if you stand in its path, you'll likely become roadkill.

Sure, you can exert influence on some situations, but don't expect circumstances to remain static or controllable. Be prepared. Learn how to adapt when the road you're on takes a sudden, unforeseen sharp turn. When the unexpected occurs, you will need to respond with speed and decisiveness.

In today's hypercompetitive and ever-changing world, we are confronted with both challenges and opportunities. In business, many people blindly follow the same playbook over and over. This is a trap because the underlying components of success may change; business models can become obsolete within months. Barriers to enter new markets have eroded with the proliferation of agile development, new technology platforms, greater data capabilities, and vendors that can seamlessly supply needed services and infrastructure. Arguably, the one sustainable competitive advantage a company possesses is the ability to stay one step ahead of its competition. And an excellent strategy to accomplish this is by embracing change.

Entrepreneurs and startups tend to be more adaptable than established companies. It's in their DNA. They understand that there will be business failures along the way, but that embracing change will open up new opportunities and increase profits. They will not to hesitate to cannibalize an existing product and create a new one to take its place.

Larger, established firms tend to be more inflexible due to several factors: company politics, lack of alignment, restrictive legacy systems, hierarchical organizations, and cultures that eschew change. Despite these formidable challenges, there is good news for larger firms. The same advances in process and technology that have eroded barriers to market entry have also made it much easier for any company to respond to change. Think of it as the democratization of change.

The real challenge faced by companies is how to balance the old and new.

Netflix is an excellent example of a company that has evolved and continues to thrive. Its leaders' keen awareness of emerging technology and consumer preferences influenced key adjustments in the company's strategy over the past decade. Netflix started out in 1998 by renting and selling DVDs via mail. In 1999, the company launched its subscription model, and in 2000, it shed the single-rental model. With improvement in bandwidth and data speeds, the company developed the "Netflix box" to deliver movie downloads into homes. Although the product was close to launch, the company leadership recognized the popularity of YouTube and altered course, introducing a streaming service in 2007. By the end of 2016, Netflix enabled subscribers to download content and watch it offline on any device.

The company's management also understood that original content has become an important component of media companies' business. Entering the content-production industry in 2012, Netflix has dramatically grown its library of original content. This includes original series, specials, miniseries, documentaries, and feature films. Netflix's original content has been a huge success. In 2018, its productions were nominated for 112 Emmys, more than those of any other network. Today, the company operates in over 190 countries and has more than 130 million subscribers.

Compare Netflix to its one-time more successful competitor, Blockbuster. Blockbuster had an extensive brick-and-mortar business for the distribution and rental of movies and games. But the company was slow to acknowledge and respond to the growing demand for streaming media. It took a different path, and by the time its leadership understood the shift in the marketplace, it was too late.

Netflix did have some missteps along the way, but its leaders responded. For example, in 2011, they announced they would split the company into a streaming service and a DVD-by-mail service. This lead to criticism, as it would require customers to use separate accounts, preferences, and websites—and it would entail higher fees. Customers were vocal; they did not want more cost and complexity. In response to the criticism, Netflix's leaders reversed their decision.

Netflix is a textbook lesson of how a company should evolve its business model in response to changing technology and customer preferences.

Advances in technology have long powered innovation. Some people or companies cannot or will not keep up with these changes for a variety of reasons. It may be that what they do works. They aren't interested in new methods, or they don't fully understand the value that those methods offer. New technology can create unwanted disruption, and no matter how beneficial, adopting it can be far more difficult than doing nothing.

Individuals who are resistant to change can generally be divided into two categories:

1. People who are not capable of adapting to change and will resist.

2. People who accept that change is needed but won't embrace it if they can't control it.

If a leader falls into one of these categories, they can derail the best-intentioned initiatives for all the wrong reasons. The second category can be particularly disappointing to deal with. These leaders will readily accept innovative concepts if those concepts come from them or their team members. However, they criticize or suppress ideas that come from other teams. This "not invented here" strategy can be rooted in selfishness or insecurity. It ultimately hurts a company's performance, creating a culture of animosity and distrust.

I have witnessed a situation in which a leader worked overtly and covertly to derail a project. They explicitly told their team to deprioritize the project, despite the fact that it was a company priority. In broader meetings, they communicated their wholehearted support and commitment to the project. This created plausible deniability; they could point to their support while applying the brakes behind closed doors. In a subsequent reorganization, this same leader was given responsibility for the project. You can probably guess how this story ends. The leader did a 180 and embraced the project. Suddenly, the brick walls they'd built came tumbling down and the project was put on the fast track.

In some circumstances, senior leaders are themselves comfortable with change, but they recognize that new initiatives can be viewed as a threat from within the company. It's a tough choice between swimming against the current and towing the line. In an effort to allay the fears of their peers, they may downplay their enthusiasm for a project. They may even malign the initiative with the intent to prevent it from moving forward. Success becomes a casualty of fear and pressure. In this scenario, personal survival comes at a cost to the company.

This scenario can create frustration for those eager to move a new initiative forward. In extreme cases, the conflicts that arise from these situations can splinter teams and lead to lasting negative consequences for the company's culture.

You may be faced with opposition when introducing innovative thinking, and it's important to understand the tactics you can employ in these situations.

Perhaps the most effective response is to show how the change will support—or even accelerate—business goals. Build the appropriate business case, and use supporting documentation to link concepts to outcomes. Focus on understanding what is important to your target audience (your prospects or clients). Use research or focus groups to corroborate the desirability of a new product or service. It is hard to refute that being responsive to customer needs is good for business. The corporate graveyard is full of companies that consciously decided to ignore the signals and failed to deliver on customer needs.

Another effective tactic is to look at industry trends. Highlight specific examples of how competitors or other industries have been successful. In some cases, a company will only launch a new product or service if a competitor successfully does it first. Opinions will change when it can be shown that others are achieving success.

It is always harder to resist innovation and change if they can be linked back to desired business objectives and greater customer satisfaction.

Embracing change means being prepared for it. It's important to anticipate unforeseen scenarios and be ready to mitigate any problems. Do you have a game plan for when the unexpected happens?

I worked with a fantastic leader who created a yearly planning process that required contingency planning and sunset provisions for each of our funded projects. If we experienced an unexpected revenue downturn or jump in expenses, we had a plan to mitigate the impact on the bottom line. Such plans could range from simply slowing down or reducing expenditures to phasing out specific projects not meeting our required return on investment. When embarking on a project, prepare for a wide range of scenarios— even those you hope won't happen. You'll be far more resilient in responding to change when you have a plan in place.

Change is not for the faint of heart; it takes conviction and fortitude to evolve and stay relevant. The road that got you to where you are today may not be the same one that takes you to the next stage. Getting too comfortable can lead to complacency... and make it more difficult to adapt in the future.

"There is nothing permanent except change."

—*Heraclitus*

~ ~

Chapter 6

DOORS WILL CLOSE UNEXPECTEDLY, BUT EVEN MORE DOORS WILL OPEN.

"Opportunity is missed by most people because it is dressed in overalls and looks like work."

—*Anonymous*

SHIT HAPPENS! IT may not be the most elegant phrase to describe the way life throws unexpected events at you, but it's a fact. Our professional lives are full of abrupt changes that can happen at the most inopportune times. Reorganizations, downsizing, outsourcing, automation or AI replacement, relocations, and changes in leadership have become so common nearly everyone encounters them at some point. These events will test and shape you, and your responses to them can change the way others think about you.

When I was halfway through my first rotation in a bank management development program, my boss called me into his office. He had a serious look on his face; I couldn't imagine what he was going to tell me. He explained that 10 percent of the colleagues I worked with would be getting laid off and leaving the building immediately. I'd been in the corporate world for less than six months. I was in shock. "Unfortunately," he said, "this is something that you and your generation will very likely experience throughout your career."

He was right.

This happened at a time when most companies had an unspoken rule of lifetime employment. It may be hard to imagine today, but there was a time when people started their career with a company and expected to retire with that same company. In fact, there was a stigma associated with being laid off. People would assume it was due to low performance, and it often became an obstacle to finding a new job.

Today's corporate culture is rife with layoffs. Employees are much more acclimated to the inherent uncertainty of their jobs, and company loyalty has largely disappeared. Not surprisingly, this serial layoff culture has led to the rise of the perennial passive job seeker. Many people are open to discussing potential new opportunities even when they're satisfied with their current role or company. As the saying goes, "The best time to find a job is when you have one."

Unless you're incredibly lucky, you will experience at least one layoff or change in role that forces you to look for a new job. There may be times preceding such an event when your intuition sends off a warning, but recognize that you can also be blindsided. You may have a good reputation and solid performance reviews. But working hard and being successful doesn't always lead to recognition and advancement.

What should you do if it happens to you? The first thing you should do, and it is difficult, is to not take it personally. Events that affect you may not seem fair, and in some cases, they aren't. Quickly put these events behind you, and don't stare in the rearview mirror. Remember that others will be watching and how you choose to respond will get their attention. Pouting or complaining will be considered immature behavior. Doing so can close the door on other opportunities within the company.

Focusing on the future is the best approach you can take. As bleak as things may seem, you can always count on new doors opening and presenting opportunities for the next chapter in your career.

The next step is to craft a plan to guide you through the transition. Understand your options, timing, and priorities. Decide on the roles you desire and companies you want to work for. Once you have prioritized these, be prepared to communicate this information to others. Create a one-page personal profile that will help others understand exactly what your career goals are. This is different from a resume or CV. A resume or CV is a recap of your experience, education, and awards. A personal profile details the roles you are interested in, your core strengths, and what kinds of companies you want to work for. The sections should include:

- Brief career summary
- Three to four career highlights with brief summaries
- Specialties and skills
- Target positions

- Target company profiles
- Specific list of targeted companies

As you look for a new position, ask questions. Can you envision where this job will lead, what your next role might be? Will the new job give you the potential for career advancement? Will it expand your skills or expose you to new responsibilities? Is the company an industry leader? Are employee reviews of the culture and leadership favorable?

It's important to be prepared—to have a game plan for handling the unexpected. Your goal should be to give yourself options. The last thing you want to do is make a hasty decision that takes you from one difficult situation into another. It may be hard to turn down a job, but it will be far more difficult in the long term to accept one that you really don't want.

Your plan will vary based on the circumstances, including your financial resources and job market conditions. Here is a mini–survival guide to get you started:

- **Be financially prepared** – I've read that saving the equivalent of three months of expenses is a good benchmark. I don't agree; six to twelve months is a more appropriate amount to see you through a transition. It's difficult to save money, let alone to save enough to cover a year's worth of expenses, but this is your best insurance against being forced to make undesirable career choices.

- **Become a passive job seeker** – Know your worth for comparable roles. Stay current on what jobs or skills are in demand. Look into compensation of your skills and experience level at other companies, or work with a recruiter.

Information, like savings, is a crucial hedge to hasty decisions that come from unexpected situations and change.

- **Network 24/7** – Continuously connect with members of your network. Your network consists of former colleagues, recruiters, friends, or others you've met in professional settings. Know who the key members in your network are, and which of them you can rely on if needed. Ensure that your social media profiles and resume/CV are professionally written, proofed, and current. Be sure to include the appropriate keywords and skills for the roles you are most interested in finding. Offer to help others when they go through their own transitions.

- **Know what you want** – Whether employed or in transition, think about what types of roles you are willing to consider. Are you willing to change industries? Can you relocate? Are you willing to take a reduction in compensation for the right role? Do you want to start your own firm? Don't wait until a job change occurs to know these answers; revisit these questions annually.

The reality is that doors will close unexpectedly. Part of career nimbleness is being prepared to face the unknown. Make it a priority to create a financial safety net, and take a proactive approach to monitoring the job market. Have a plan to weather career detours and downturns so you won't be forced into making suboptimal decisions.

Most importantly, while you will experience stress when a door closes, be optimistic about the opportunities that will emerge when new doors open.

"Some wise person said that good luck is nothing but preparation meets opportunity. I agree. I also think that bad luck is nothing but lack of preparation meeting reality."

—*Eliyahu M. Goldratt*

Chapter 7

CONTROL WHAT YOU CAN, AND DON'T OBSESS OVER WHAT YOU CAN'T.

"You may not control all the events that happen to you, but you can decide not to be reduced by them."
—*Maya Angelou*

WE ARE CONSTANTLY affected by circumstances beyond our control. Learning how to accept and respond to events outside your control will be more effective than trying to resist or ignore them. This isn't easy, but it's an essential skill that will serve you well.

Understanding what you can or cannot control is important. This is key in how you respond when faced with adversity or unexpected events. When you have control over a situation, it will be easier for you to resolve problems. Seek out the opinions of others, but take decisive action to resolve issues. Conversely, when you're not in control, you can often influence others to make a decision.

In either situation, gather the information you need to make an informed recommendation.

The following is a list of some of the issues you might encounter:

Things you can control:

- How you manage your leader's expectations
- Your own decisions about business priorities or funding
- Your accountability for project deliverables
- Discretionary spending decisions
- Support and guidance for coworkers

Things you can't control:

- Demands from a leader
- Senior management directives
- External factors
  - * Competition
  - * New technology
  - * Shifting consumer/client preferences
- Regulatory policy, guidelines, and changes
- Legal/compliance mandates

Some of these issues must be addressed without delay. For instance, unplanned legal, regulatory, or compliance requirements must be responded to when they arise. I worked for large financial services company at a time when it had just launched company pages on several social media platforms. At the time, social media was so new that the regulators had not set up guidelines. The Financial Industry

Regulatory Authority (FINRA) requested that we share our strategy with them. Although we could not control their requirements, we did anticipate their concerns in advance. We chose to be proactive by making our new pages compliant with existing privacy regulations for other platforms. This addressed one of their main concerns: Personal information could not be shared publicly. Any interactions that required personal information were redirected to secure communication channels. We had the capability to control the content we created and how it was shared on social media. If we'd failed to build in such safeguards, the regulators would have ordered our social media activities to be shut down.

The regulators approved our use of social media. This was important; it was a new and vital component of our marketing strategy.

If you don't respond when these groups make a request, you can face severe consequences such as fines, legal repercussions, or loss of business. The best advice for these situations is to accept changes in regulations and ensure that you comply with them.

Just as you can't control industry regulations and laws, you can't control who your leaders are or what leadership styles they have. Your leaders will have their own struggles with what they control. Observe how they deal with these situations. This will help you to adapt to situations of your own.

There are leaders who micromanage every aspect of every project. They don't respond well to circumstances beyond their control, especially when those circumstances delay or change their plans. When they encounter unplanned events, they will likely push back or get frustrated. In some cases, they'll try to circumvent such situations entirely, at times placing undue pressure on others to cut corners.

For example, a leader may take a "we'll figure it out later" approach. Unfortunately, this can backfire because addressing the issue later may require significant effort.

Other managers are more flexible and respond quickly to unexpected issues that need to be addressed. They set direction and strategy, provide feedback, and delegate day-to-day decisions to their staff. They expect an immediate escalation of any critical issues that arise, and they want recommendations for resolving impasses. For example, cost overruns could threaten a project and the manager may demand that the team find a solution. If they move too slowly, the manager could make the decision for them.

Big-picture leaders, on the other hand, don't necessarily like to get into the details. They are adept at setting a vision but often defer the details to others. This lack of guidance may be intimidating to a new team member who may not have the confidence to make a decision.

Understanding the managerial style of your leader is crucial, because while you can't control your leader's style, you *can* control how you deal with it.

You might assume there is an inherent problem with a micromanager who exhibits a tendency to control others' behavior. Is this a sign of an obsessive or insecure person? Or is it the modus operandi of a genius? Some legendary leaders are manically focused control freaks with zero tolerance for people not doing things their way. Steve Jobs was this type of leader, and there are well-known stories about his attention to detail. He was obsessive about all aspects of a product, and it had to pass his scrutiny. According to his biographer Walter Isaacson, Jobs even cared about parts you couldn't see. He believed that you didn't shortchange innovation and design, and he was merciless in their pursuit. He carefully considered shapes of icons, feels of materials, shades of colors, and things most others would ignore... right down to Apple Store flooring material. He obsessed over Apple's computers, MacBooks, iPods, and iPhones, and his persistence resulted in prolific success. His obsession changed the world.

Dealing with a micromanager is difficult at best. Assume everything you do will be scrutinized. This includes the things they told you to do. One option is to run everything past the leader before you begin. Alternatively, you can get specific instructions on what to do or how to do it. In either case, it will be an exhausting process, but it will reduce your stress level in the long term.

There are other legendary leaders who have a very different style and approach than that of the micromanager. Sir Richard Branson founded the Virgin Group, which controls more than sixty companies. He can't possibly control every aspect of all of them, so he surrounds himself with highly competent people and relies on them. His style is not to micromanage every aspect of a project; rather, he trusts others to get the job done. He relishes being part of a team, celebrating successes with others and engaging them in decision-making. He recognizes his team members in his speeches and online postings. His management style is very different than Steve Jobs's, yet both of them are highly successful.

Most of us don't have the opportunity to work for a billionaire entrepreneur, but we all need to learn how to deal with our own leaders' management styles. Some leaders focus on achieving specific goals—for example, a sales number. Such a leader will be intensely focused on their team's ability to "make the numbers." If the numbers come up short, the leader won't let anyone forget it. Or you may encounter is a leader who isn't consistent. They may suddenly change their mind or contradict previous directions. It will be difficult but necessary to deal with these unexpected changes.

The managerial style of your leader will probably fall somewhere between that of a delegator and that of a micromanager. As you move up in an organization, you'll settle into your own style. The more team members you oversee, the more you'll have to pass some degree of control on to subordinates. Your management style, along with the personalities of your team and culture of your business, will influence how much control you retain, and how much you distribute across a larger team.

When I first became a manager, I tried to consider all possible outcomes, thinking I could control them. I learned this was not possible. There will be bumps in the road. Accept that reality. Trying to plan for every possible outcome is futile. Not only is it a huge time drain and distraction; it will slow down your progress. You will never be able to anticipate every possibility.

So what should you do? Stick to your game plan. Keep your focus on your goals. Adjust to changes as needed. Don't obsess over trying to control everything.

Sometimes, you may even need to consider removing yourself from a situation entirely. But don't rush into a new opportunity solely based on your desire to escape from a bad situation. Sticking out the tough periods takes guts and perseverance, but at times, doing so can help you chart a wise course.

Ultimately, you do have control in deciding what actions to take and when. If you have the misfortunate of being in a no-win situation, accept it and develop a plan to respond or move on. Focus on the future, and don't look back or second-guess yourself.

In time, you will become comfortable in learning to let go of the things that you can't control.

"We cannot control what emotions or circumstances we will experience next, but we can choose how we will respond to them."

—*Gary Zukav*

ॐ ॐ

Chapter 8

KNOW THE RISKS IN BEING DEPENDENT ON OTHERS TO ACHIEVE YOUR OBJECTIVES.

"Teamwork requires some sacrifice up front; people who work as a team have to put the collective needs of the group ahead of their individual interests."
—Patrick Lencioni

MANY ELEMENTS CONTRIBUTE to success or failure. Arguably, one of the biggest factors that impedes success is a lack of alignment in goals within a team or across a company. Your success often depends on willing, able, and ready partners who will support you. It will be difficult to deliver on goals if you are dependent on reluctant or uncooperative partners. Without that support, you can fail—even with a clear strategy, a plan to implement it, and hard work on your side.

In most instances, people will willingly work together to achieve a common goal or objective. Unfortunately, you'll also encounter people who don't want to help or simply don't care. I recall an occasion when I needed a coworker's help to implement a high-priority project. He was less than enthusiastic. Despite his reluctance, I included his team in the planning and strategy sessions. Our teams developed the budget proposal. After senior management approved the funding, we began to formalize the work plan—at which point he began questioning every aspect of it. He wanted to know the rationale behind my strategy, what my ROIs were, what I hoped to accomplish, and so on. He told me that he needed this information to determine what he would focus on and when to put it on the development schedule. He was asking about business case information, which had nothing to do with business requirements needed for the development schedule.

He was attempting to unilaterally make decisions with no regard for what the CEO and his team had already approved. It wasn't easy to contain my emotions. I was frustrated and exhausted by his antics and wanted to admonish him. In the end, I took a more rational approach. I told him that the executive team had approved this plan, but he was free to present his questions to the CEO directly. That basically ended his questioning of my team's priorities and plan. But the story didn't end there.

As time went on, he became increasingly obstinate, and getting his support continued to be a challenge. I kept his team in the loop, informing them about updates, meetings, and planning sessions even though they were unresponsive. (Later, I would find out he'd warned them not to get too involved.) When I could find a workaround that didn't rely on his team, I had no choice but to take it, even though it involved more work than should have been necessary. Over time, he became concerned that progress was being made without his team, and he ultimately re-engaged.

There are many reasons for goal dissonance and competing priorities. The strength or weakness of relationships, differing departmental goals within an organization, or varying compensation incentives can all lead to problems. So can ambiguity of roles, an absence of clearly articulated priorities, lack of coordination, or management by committee. In more extreme situations, outright obstinacy is to blame. Regardless of the reason, goal dissonance can lead to organizational dysfunction, job dissatisfaction, and animosity among coworkers. These outcomes can create a toxic culture.

Although larger companies tend to have more complex structures, firms of all sizes can experience goal dissonance. There are three levels at which goal misalignment can occur. Each has an adverse impact on overall success. Figure 1 depicts each of these levels and the degree of impact is has.

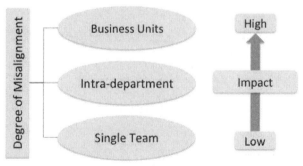

Figure 1 – Organizational Impact of Goal Misalignment

The simplest level to deal with is misaligned goals within a single team. The team's leader can often easily resolve this.

It gets more complicated when team goals across a department are not aligned. The head of the group needs to rectify differences between teams to gain alignment. If they fail to do this, teams will continue to be at odds and the department will be less likely to achieve success.

The most challenging scenario, and the one that can have the most lasting impact, is when goals across the company are not in sync. Business units can be like a group of autonomous fiefdoms. Unless there is alignment among them, you might find yourself caught between warring feudal lords, each of them pushing their own agenda.

Company leaders may believe the company has a consistent set of priorities, but unfortunately that doesn't always turn out to be the case. The stage is set for setbacks or failure when a leader sets priorities but doesn't ensure they are communicated, acknowledged, and actively supported by all groups. Companies with persistent misalignment of goals tend to have politically charged or dysfunctional cultures. They have winners and losers.

An effective approach to improving your likelihood of success with others is to build strong relationships. This makes it easier to find common ground. Proactively reach out to others to open a dialog and share expectations. Clear communication and transparency will foster strong relationships and trust with coworkers.

If you are having difficulty in aligning goals, take a direct approach. This means:

- Arrange in-person discussions
- Highlight mutual goals and objectives
- Keep lines of communication open
- Set up regular updates to track progress

Be constructive, honest, and direct without allowing emotions to get the best of you. Separate out personality issues if they exist, and use facts to show your coworker(s) how alignment is a win-win. Let them know you value the partnership. Regardless of any personality conflicts, always be respectful.

If you still can't resolve the situation, then escalate it to your leader. Often leaders will encourage you to resolve issues on your own, but there will be times when you need to enlist their help.

If all else fails, you will have no other choice but to seek alternative routes to work around the obstacles. Depending on which group you are at an impasse with, it may be difficult—even impossible—to find an alternative solution. In this case, communicate with those who are not willing or able to work with you, and be clear about the impact their actions will have on the project. Keep your leader informed throughout the process. If you are unsuccessful in getting their assistance, you'll need to reset your timelines and expectations.

While individual performance will be a major factor in your accomplishments, be aware that your success will likely depend on others' willingness to work with you. Build good relationships, and if confronted with key partners who cannot or will not work with you, look for alternatives or escalate to your leader. Also be mindful that others may rely on you and your team to support their objectives. If you can't give them your full support, be candid and clear on what is and is not possible. Be open to collaboration and contributing to others' success. Always aim for win-win situations.

"Be wary of the man who urges an action in which he himself incurs no risk."

—*Joaquin Setanti*

---

෨   ෫

Chapter 9

PERFECTIONISM CAN BE A CURSE; LEARN WHEN GOOD IS ENOUGH.

"Courage is going from failure to failure without losing enthusiasm."

—*Anonymous*

GETTING IT RIGHT is important, but getting it perfect can derail you from achieving your goals. Perfectionists like Elon Musk and Steven Spielberg create enormous success despite the wakes of disruption they often leave in their paths. Perfectionists lost to obscurity, however, vastly outnumber these legendary leaders. And perfectionists can be their own worst enemies. Serena Williams is a self-described perfectionist, and no one is tougher on her than her. Despite her enormous success, she believes there are many things she can improve on. Her frustration in not living up to her own very high standards at times leads to smashed rackets and lost games.

Are you a perfectionist? How would you know if you were? Chances are you're one if everything you do could be better or if you are incessantly trying to "get it right." And it's not only major things; it can be something minor. Writing an email, giving a presentation, or conveying a point can all fall victim to perfectionism. Being obsessive makes it hard to think in terms of "good enough." This can undermine your confidence because you will always have a feeling of coming up short. Another consequence of perfectionism is that tasks will often take much longer than they should. It's better to try to get a project good enough, and if it falls short, use that as a lesson on how to make it better next time.

Finding the situations when "good enough" is acceptable is a balancing act, and there are a number of variables involved. Take product development, for instance. Aiming for perfection during the product development process can torpedo success by inflating costs, increasing time to market, or driving the development of features that customers don't really want or need.

Sony introduced its Betamax videocassette in the mid-1970s. The format was superior to its rival, VHS. However, VHS offered an open format that was more widely adopted by manufacturers. Eventually Sony discontinued the Betamax format in favor of VHS.

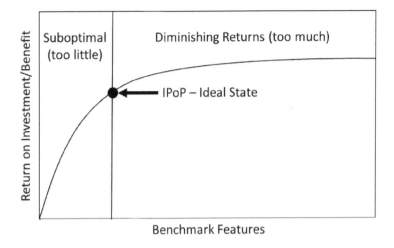

Figure 2 – Inflection Point of Perfection (IPoP)

How do you know when "good" is sufficient to launch a product or service? It takes a 360-degree perspective to understand all the complexities involved. High-performing companies discern the difference of when it is essential to be best in class and when parity is acceptable. Delivering a perfect product or service should be an aspirational guide; it may be acceptable to launch short of the ideal state and evolve toward it over time. When creating a product, it's important to consider the law of diminishing returns. As Investopedia explains, "At some point, adding an additional factor of production results in smaller increases in output."[1] What I term the inflection point of perfection (IPoP) can be defined as the optimal delivery state of a product or service (see Figure 2). Points along the continuum before the IPoP is reached represent a suboptimal product or service, meaning that features or functionality of core components

---

1 Investopedia. "Law of Diminishing Marginal Returns." Last modified May 22, 2018. https://www.investopedia.com/terms/l/lawofdiminishingmarginalreturn. asp.

aren't fully developed. Any point beyond the IPoP represents efforts that will result in smaller returns. The challenging part, of course, is recognizing what the IPoP is and when you get there.

Start with defining what the IPoP is, and then develop a data set to serve as a guide. This should include the following key categories:

- **Client need:** Is internal thinking—the company's perspective, not the client's—used to make decisions? Are you building something that meets an explicit or latent customer need? Latent needs are those features or functionalities that clients would value but don't explicitly express a need for. For example, it's been claimed that Henry Ford said, "If I had asked people what they wanted, they would have said faster horses."

  Ethnography, which is a part of social anthropology, is an invaluable technique that uses primary field research to study people in their everyday environments. By direct observation, a researcher uncovers what product features or functionalities would be valued by their target audience. Ethnography may be the reason Chrysler put cup holders in the first minivans, which (like cup holders) they invented in 1983. Today, cup holders are an essential feature in cars, SUVs, minivans, and pickup trucks.

- **Competitive benchmark:** An important aspect of product development is having a keen understanding of the competition. Do you know who your core competitors are? How do your firm's products or services compare on features and functionality?

  Competitive pressure is a key driver of innovation and product improvement. But it's important to know when to create competitive parity and when to create a best-in-class product or service. There are certain aspects of a product for which meeting a competitive standard is perfectly fine. Conversely, there are other aspects where a creating a clearly distinctive competitive advantage is appropriate.

Knowing the difference between the two will enable you to focus on the most relevant needs of your customers. It takes some thought and fact-finding to determine the difference between them. For example, an auto manufacturer would benefit from having best-in-class safety features to protect passengers. It should not come as a surprise that consumers place a value on safety features and will pay a premium for them. This benefit would not, however, extend to crafting the best sun visors.

- **Cost-benefit analysis:** If an investment requires millions of dollars, yet results only in a small return, then why proceed? Under these circumstances, it makes sense to put the money to better use and garner higher returns. Examine both the short-term and long-term benefits; the latter represents a more strategic priority. Although there are a variety of metrics to evaluate investments, your company may require you to use specific ones.

  Two metrics you should consider are net present value (NPV) and breakeven analysis. NPV is the net present value of cash flows (revenue minus expenses) over time. It is adjusted by a discount rate, which is used to adjust future dollars into today's value. NPV is a great long-term value measurement, but be certain to prioritize investments that have reasonably good cash-flow projections in the early years. Investments that have a higher proportion of cash flows in the later years are riskier because they are more uncertain.

In breakeven analysis, the breakeven point is simply the point in time at which the revenue earned equals the costs incurred. Lower breakeven points are good indicators, but they do not necessarily mean the associated projects will be the most profitable ones.

Over the past decade, there has been a considerable shift in how companies bring new products and services to market. The traditional software development method—called the waterfall method—typically takes a one-direction approach. According to TechRepublic, the waterfall method "is a framework for software development in which development proceeds sequentially through a series of phases, starting with system requirements analysis and leading up to product release and maintenance."[2] Because of the sequential process, the waterfall method is inflexible; it can be challenging to perform course corrections. This can increase the likelihood of launch delays, budget overruns, or coming up short on required features or functionality. Conversely, an advantage of this process is that business requirements must be clearly defined up front by all involved parties.

The newer method is known as agile development. This approach is driven by an iterative development process that relies on close collaboration of team members throughout the life cycle of the project. The development and business teams stay in close communication

2 Contributor Melonfire. "Understanding the Pros and Cons of the Waterfall Model of Software Development." TechRepublic, September 22, 2006. https://www.techrepublic.com/article/understanding-the-pros-and-cons-of-the-waterfall-model-of-software-development/.

and address issues as they come up. Agile development is a flexible and nimble method with a common-sense approach: an iterative process that tackles launches in stages, allowing for course correcting as needed. Trying to get things right the first time through the less pliable waterfall process is a risky proposition.

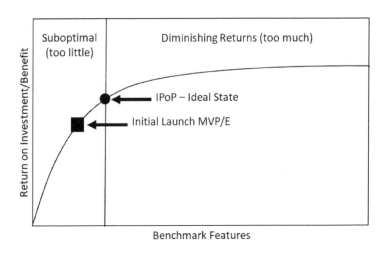

Figure 3 – Minimally Viable Product/Experience (MVP/E)

To stay on track, product development needs to have a clearly defined project roadmap. Start with the research; understand your priorities and what it will take to create a minimally viable product (MVP), also referred to as a minimally viable experience (MVE). When you aim for a MVP/E, your goal is to get a product to market with baseline features. Keep in mind that future enhancements will be needed. As depicted in Figure 3, an initial launch of a MVP/E is not at the ideal IPoP. Implementing enhancements postlaunch will get you to the ideal state.

Launching a MVP/E cannot be done in a vacuum. Without an initial understanding of future requirements, there's a risk that future development will be skipped—or costly to implement. A drawback with MVP/E is that companies tend to launch a product and move on without building the necessary future enhancements that were identified during the gathering of requirements. This will leave gaps which, if not addressed, result in a less-than-competitive product or service.

Don't fall prey to this MVP/E shortcoming. The MVP/E is only a starting point. Continuous improvement is necessary throughout the product life cycle in order to be competitive and maintain customer loyalty.

Once the IPoP is defined, another important decision company leaders need to make is whether the company should be a first mover or a fast follower. A first mover is the company that is the first to launch a new product or service. Such companies gain an advantage by being first and will typically establish strong brand recognition and customer loyalty. A fast follower will typically take a "wait and see" approach. If a first mover is successful, fast followers will quickly launch their own versions of the product or service and try to leapfrog the first mover.

Startups are typically first movers because they create new business models or processes that challenge existing companies. Their innovation can be perceived as perfection, but is it? When Amazon launched its online book business, some might have thought Jeff Bezos had come up with the perfect model. At the time, maybe it was. But Amazon has continuously evolved and continued to improve its business, expanding beyond its starting point.

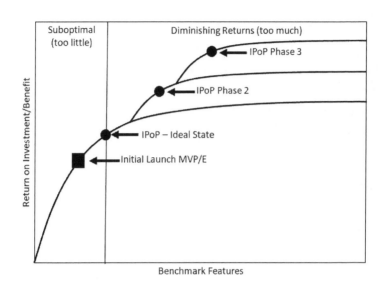

Figure 4 – Multiphase Minimally Viable Product/Experience (MVP/E)

The IPoP can shift in time due to new technology and capabilities that drive new business models. Companies don't typically launch products and services at the IPoP, but they understand the need to get there. However, as a company's business model evolves, its leaders need to reset the IPoP for the next business stage. Figure 4 depicts this multiphase scenario, where IPoPs change in lockstep with new business stages. The process is dynamic and continues to evolve as the business does.

Companies often struggle between starting with good enough and aiming for perfection. These days, firms typically launch a MVP/E and go through successive upgrades to get closer to the perfect product or service. Long-term winners know how to start with "good enough" and remain responsive to change as needed. Good, not perfect, is their starting point, and they become great in time by focusing on their long-term objectives.

"Striving for excellence motivates you; striving for perfection is demoralizing."

—*Harriet Braiker*

Chapter 10

FOLLOW YOUR PASSION.

"It takes courage to grow up and become who you really are."

—E. E. Cummings

THE HARDEST DECISION you will likely make during your career is choosing the right role(s) or career path. Understanding the difference between what you want to do (passion) and what you're good at (competence) is critical to career success and ultimate happiness. For some of you, passion and competency are the same. For others, your passion may not be aligned to what you're competent at doing. And there will be yet others for whom what you do is not your passion. Finding the right balance between passion and competency can be frustrating, but it's worth the effort.

You may have heard the saying, "If you love what you do, it isn't work." This is a truth you can count on. People who love what they do are happier and more satisfied than those who dislike their jobs. Who wouldn't want a job that is rewarding and enjoyable—a job that they're passionate about?

If you're enamored with your job and also competent at it, congratulations! You're one of the few who have attained career nirvana. For the majority of us who have not been as lucky, don't despair. It's never too late to reassess and focus on finding the ideal combination of passion and competency. Don't expect to find an instant solution; you need to set your target and work diligently to get there. Prolific musicians like Paul McCartney, Bruce Springsteen and Jay-Z didn't start out as superstars, but they knew music was their destiny. Like other successful people who fell in love with a profession, they worked tirelessly in pursuit of their dreams with passion and determination. In fact, they made significant sacrifices, faced personal challenges, and risked failure along the way.

Bruce Springsteen has said, "When I was growing up, there were two things that were unpopular in my house. One was me and the other was my guitar." He hit it big in 1975 with the release of *Born to Run*, reaching number three on the Billboard 200. While his story is one of rags to riches, thousands more with the same passion will not find the same success. This doesn't diminish their passion for music. In fact, many find happiness playing in local bands, making YouTube videos, or composing in their leisure time.

There are stories of others who leave seemingly successful careers to pursue their passions; Ken Jeong is one such person. He grew up loving comedy and comedians, but his parents, not surprisingly, wanted him to pursue a stable career. He graduated from the University of North Carolina School of Medicine at Chapel Hill in 1995 and began his residency in New Orleans. During this time, he moonlighted as a comedian performing at local clubs and loved it. After he won a local comedy contest, he got the attention of others who encouraged him to move to Los Angeles. There he practiced medicine for over seven years and continued to hone his comedy skills. He appeared on ABC's *The View* and acquired a reputation for being a doctor with a sense of humor. He went on to becoming a full time comedian with success in movies, TV, commercials, and as a spokesperson.

Similarly, many entrepreneurs are willing to work tirelessly in pursuit of their passion. They drain all their financial resources, max out credit cards, and move into their offices to save on rent. Despite long odds, passion fuels a relentless drive to achieve success.

How do you know if you're doing what you love as opposed to simply what you're good at doing? The choices you will face are complicated, and there will sometimes be a tug of war between rational and emotional considerations. Great compensation or perks can lure us into believing that we are passionate about a particular role. But good compensation doesn't guarantee the best career option in the long term.

The Want-Competency Matrix (Table 2) is a framework to help you evaluate the desirability or fit of a specific role or career path. It's important that you objectively determine each factor for your current role (or one you want). Keep in mind that your placement in one quadrant today does not mean you'll be there forever. Where you fall on this matrix can change over time for a number of reasons, including having a clearer understanding of your goals and developing competencies that come with experience.

		Competency	
		Low	High
Want	High	Develop	Desired
	Low	Avoid	Reassess

Table 2 – Want-Competency Matrix

High Want/High Competency (Desired): The ideal state is when both a high want and high competency exists. These roles offer you a high level of satisfaction, and you have the prerequisite skills necessary for the position. People who have or find a job in this quadrant are most likely, on average, to be both satisfied and successful.

High Want/Low Competency (Develop): This quadrant presents a conundrum for individuals who desire a specific role but lack some of the prerequisite skills needed for the position. The most obvious course of action is to take training classes to close gaps. You can take a position that fits into this quadrant, because with experience your competency level will rise—promotions often fall into this bucket. Leaders understand that there will be growth in the new role.

Low Want/High Competency (Reassess): Positions that fall into this quadrant are jobs that match your skill set—you are (or would be) very good at them. However, your low level of desire for these roles could become a source of dissatisfaction and adversely impact your long-term performance. If you're in a role or considering one in this quadrant, the question you must ask yourself is whether or not your passion and motivation for the job can improve. Good compensation may cloud your judgment. In making a decision, you need to separate income from job satisfaction.

Low Want/Low Competency (Avoid): These roles should be avoided at all costs. If you find yourself in this quadrant or looking at a role that falls into it, focus your efforts on finding a role better suited for you.

There's a balance between finding the role you passionately want and finding one that you're capable of performing in at a high level. Remember, if you don't have all the skills you need for a role, that doesn't necessarily mean that you should forgo it. Determine what steps you need to take to close any gaps, whether those are on-the-job training, taking additional classes, or finding a mentor to help you through the transition.

Your career path will not always follow an upward trajectory. Taking a detour today to build needed skills can pay off in big ways down the road. Focus on the roles that spark your passion and motivate you; don't be sidetracked by the short-term allure of compensation. Even if it means initially accepting roles with lower pay, over the long run this strategy will pay off.

Over the past six decades, a variety of studies have shown a high correlation between job satisfaction and job performance. It shouldn't come as a surprise that low job satisfaction can lead to higher turnover rates, absenteeism, or lack of engagement—even for roles where a high competency exists. Lack of motivation is a powerful force that weighs down productivity and creativity, creating an undercurrent of mediocre performance. There is also a significant risk that a disinterested employee's performance could have a negative influence on coworkers. Companies may not always recognize a discernible effect on the firm, but make no mistake: your lack of engagement will adversely affect others and reduce their productivity.

On the other side of the spectrum, passion is a motivator that increases job satisfaction. This in turn creates benefits that can permeate throughout the company, producing better problem-solving and collaboration. People who are passionate tend to be willing to help and foster camaraderie with others. Over the long term, a company with highly satisfied employees will have a competitive advantage.

In reality, no company has 100 percent highly satisfied employees. However, if leaders create the appropriate culture and incentives, employees are much more likely to be content. Ways to foster a high-performing culture include empowerment, mutual respect, coaching, and giving employees a voice. If management makes the commitment and invests the resources to maintain high employee satisfaction, those leaders will be rewarded with above average growth.

You may have heard stories of people who had a "dream job" and were earning a large salary—and unexpectedly quit. Many of them were simply not happy, and they decided to pursue a more fulfilling career. Among the reasons they cite are a loathing for their work, being part of an undesirable culture, and mostly not having a feeling of satisfaction. They yearn to do mission-based work, seeking roles that will provide them with greater satisfaction or create purpose in their lives. Despite the likelihood of a drastic drop in short-term income, there's evidence that people who make dramatic career changes in pursuit of fulfillment end up happier over the long run. (To be fair, some suggest they may not—a position I don't agree with.)

Making career choices is seldom simple. When considering a new role or venture, understand the risks. Be thoughtful when considering whether to choose a role that's safe or pays well rather than focusing on one that drives you. Sometimes it's wise to settle for a safe role because it provides the security you seek. For example, if others are financially dependent on you, pursuing a startup opportunity may be too risky. Another factor to take into account is whether a role provides the work-life balance you desire. In today's hyper-competitive world, many roles require you to be plugged in 24/7. If you aspire to such a role, make sure it's one you'll love.

Seek roles that are well aligned with your skills and talents. Invest the time to find the right balance of passion and competency. Passion is the navigation system for a successful and satisfying career, and competency is the thrust to propel you to new levels. Be true to yourself, and reach for the stars.

"Good judgment comes from experience—and a lot of that comes from bad judgment."

—*Anonymous*

Chapter 11

ALWAYS EMBRACE THE SPIRIT OF DISCOVERY AND INNOVATION.

"Innovation is the creation of the new or the re-arranging of the old in a new way."

—*Michael Vance*

CHANGE IS SCARY, but inevitable. Throughout history, great thinkers have often been ridiculed—and sometimes punished, jailed, or killed—for introducing change. Galileo spent years of his life under house arrest after he challenged the common belief that the earth was at the center of the universe and the sun revolved around it. It's hard to believe today that this was considered an existential threat to prevailing beliefs of his time. But people are predisposed to stick with what works or what is already accepted as true. As the saying goes, "If it ain't broke, don't fix it."

Typically the path of least resistance boils down to doing nothing, even if you believe change is needed. Maybe people find it difficult to accept change because they have already invested time and resources into a process or product. They feel that changing course could be seen as waffling. Or maybe they feel threatened by the change and can't easily move in a new direction. Change makes people nervous.

One of the toughest challenges a company can face is determining whether its current employees have the skills to get it to the next level. Another challenge is the added cost (or demand on resources) that a change in direction creates. In many cases, during a transition, the company will have to pay for both the existing system and the new system for an extended period of time. Transitions generally include a variety of testing, quality control, development, and retraining before the eventual decommissioning of the original system. It should come as no surprise that legacy systems become a competitive impediment. New entrants without those constraints can launch innovative offerings more easily.

There is a long list of one-time household names that went out of business because they failed to respond to innovation or could not evolve. Kodak's Steve Sasson invented the digital camera in 1975, and the company patented it in 1978. However, the company made most of its sales from traditional photography and waited too long to shift to digital. Wang Laboratories created the first word processor, but it was displaced by the personal computer, which possessed more software flexibility. Eventually Microsoft took over the operating system space with its Windows software and integrated Office products. Established retailers are stumbling with the rise of online shopping, which has put many decades-old brands on the corporate endangered list.

What if these companies had embraced innovation? It's safe to say that these stories would have had different endings.

"Great spirits have always encountered violent opposition from mediocre minds."

—*Albert Einstein*

Merriam-Webster defines innovation as "a new idea, method, or device."[3] In business, this includes the process of improving or transforming an existing process or product. It is driven by ingenuity, technology, and a propensity to respond to unmet customer needs. Progressive companies seek to understand the impact that innovation and trends have on their business models.

Through the 1970s, telephone companies were very profitable and faced little competition, so there wasn't much incentive to innovate. With the breakup of the Ma Bell monopoly into smaller regional companies, product and service innovation began. The companies adopted technology that turned tethered rotary phones with limited capabilities into phones and networks with more functionality. For a time, regional companies continued to maintain market dominance, but this too gave way to new competitive pressures. Our lives were forever changed by the innovations that lead to the creation of high-speed cellular networks and mobile devices. Today, the descendants of Ma Bell—like Verizon and AT&T—have morphed into

---

3 Merriam-Webster Online. "innovation." Accessed December 22, 2018. https://www.merriam-webster.com/dictionary/innovation.

diverse communications companies and offer services like cable and satellite TV.

One of the most memorable stories that highlights just how strong the resistance to innovation can be comes from American Express. The story dates back to the 1950s, and it's a lesson on the foresight and the bravery that it took to invest in a new product—a product that was perceived as a threat to the company's flagship traveler's check business. What was this new, dangerous innovation that threatened the existence of the company?

It was the charge card.

As Reference for Business describes the events:

When Diners Club introduced the first credit card in the mid-1950s, American Express executives proposed investigating this new line of business. [President] Reed, who thought the company should improve existing business and feared a credit card would threaten its traveler's check business, opposed the proposal. In 1958, Reed reversed himself and the American Express travel-and-entertainment card (the American Express green card) was introduced virtually overnight. The company had 250,000 to 300,000 applications for cards on hand the day the card went on the market, and 500,000 card members within three months. Introduction of the green card began an era of unprecedented growth: earnings rose from $8.4 million in 1959 to $85 million in 1970.[4]

---

4 Reference for Business. "American Express Company—Company Profile, Information, Business Description, History, Background Information on American Express Company." Accessed December 22, 2018. http://www.refer-enceforbusiness.com/history2/67/American-Express-Company.html.

Had the company not embraced change, there's a reasonable possibility that it would have faded into the annals of corporate history. Instead, it thrived and became one of the world's preeminent brands, with tens of millions of card members. Yes, a small piece of plastic turned out to be an innovation that catapulted the company into an era of profitability and growth.

Innovation takes guts; innovators have to be brave to challenge the status quo by advocating for an unproven product or service. It's hard to support an idea that is viewed as a risk or a threat to a core business model. The wall of resistance is formidable, and in some cases, it even sidetracks an innovator's career.

Innovators are also curious. They want to know how the pieces fit together, why things are done a certain way, where they can be done differently. They don't like hearing "that's the way we've always done it," and they will deconstruct processes and transform them. These are some reasons why others may view innovators as unwanted interlopers or disruptors. They fear innovators may expose the current methods or systems as inefficient. They would rather not "rock the boat," even if that means inefficiencies will not be addressed.

People often misconstrue innovators' curiosity and become suspicious about their motives. However, most innovators' motives are straightforward. They have a passion to improve products and services that will retain and win new customers. Unfortunately, all too often they become targets for insecure coworkers, who block their paths. Many either give up or take their ideas elsewhere to develop.

It's logical that one can't just go out and create a broad array of changes and innovation without creating disruption—and it's important to be realistic about that. Innovative people must understand that their passion to invent can put people off. To ignore these reactions is to risk failure. The best option to avert this outcome is to spend time linking new ideas to business outcomes. It may not win converts, but demonstrating how the business can benefit is a sound tactic to gain traction. Innovation shouldn't be the enemy of tradition, nor should it be suppressed out of fear. Resistance leads to mediocrity. Entrenched, mediocre minds can have a chilling effect on change.

There are several tactics companies can deploy to assuage the objections of naysayers. First, companies should embrace innovation and encourage their employees to take some risks. Risk is not a bad word and should not be confused with recklessness. A company will benefit from innovation if it creates a culture that accepts innovation. Second, companies may create skunk works or innovation labs as standalone businesses within the company. (A skunk works team is a small group of people who operate outside the mainstream business; it may have its own budget, technology, and location.) This approach is designed to prevent legacy systems and company politics from derailing innovation. Third, firms can fund, invest in, or partner with start-ups or other disruptors to fast-track products and services without interference from existing business lines. Alternately, some businesses create a joint venture or acquire a company that provides a desirable service or product. For example, in 2013, PayPal purchased Venmo, an innovative person-to-person payment provider that had gained traction with younger users. While PayPal could have tried to create a competitive offering, in this instance it was easier to purchase the challenger.

Innovation works best when the initial ideation ignores all impediments such as funding and technology barriers. Why? Because this kind of thinking is focused on designing ideal features and functionality free of preconceived limitations. Once this is done, you can address any real-world issues. Another important part of innovation is to define sunset provisions—a time to pull the plug, should performance not meet expectations. Not all innovation leads to success, and failure is compounded when you don't know when to throw in the towel.

A business culture that embraces the spirit of discovery promotes innovation. It supports calculated risks, accepts challenging the status quo, relies on key performance indicators (KPIs), and has a strong governance model. If working in an innovative culture appeals to you, seek out a leader or company that encourages the exploration of new ideas. Look for characteristics such as flexibility, adaptability, risk-taking, communications, and teamwork.

Although innovation should not be viewed as the enemy, you should also respect the current paradigm. It may have a strong, reliable track record, but it may not be enough to carry the company to the next level. Any transition will be fraught with challenges and adjustments. Innovators will often be met with resistance and barriers, but perseverance and a maniacal focus on driving change can pay off. Embrace the spirit of discovery and seek out what might be possible without focusing on constraints and barriers. Find a culture that permits its employees to be creative and explore what is possible. Tie innovation to business outcomes—that's how you'll be best prepared to create breakthrough products or services.

Chapter 12

FIND YOUR ADVOCATES; THEY WILL SUPPORT YOU AND BRING YOU WITH THEM.

"Surround yourself with people who lift you higher."
—*Oprah Winfrey*

THROUGHOUT YOUR CAREER, you will meet all types of people: smart, supportive, combative, collaborative, passionate, visionary, etc. Advocates will play a pivotal role in your development. You're not guaranteed to have an advocate; sometimes one finds you, and at other times, you find one. You'll hit the jackpot if you find an advocate who will help in your development, challenge you to excel, and bring you with them as they move up. Typically advocates are direct leaders, but they can also be coworkers, friends, peers, or even the people you manage.

Advocacy has several components, and understanding each will be essential to harnessing its potential. The first level is providing guidance. This can range from feedback on your presentation style to editing a written proposal. The second level is personal development; feedback becomes much more structured and can include a performance review, development plan, or other development tools such as personality tests. The third level is the zenith of advocacy: proactive support and mentoring. This level consists of a hands-on approach to coaching and development. All levels of advocacy can lead to benefits such as broader responsibilities, promotions, management of larger teams, assignment to mission-critical projects, or career advancement. And of course, these benefits will lead to higher pay and overall compensation.

What steps should you take to find an advocate? Start by identifying what you hope to achieve and the people who can provide advice and guidance. Typically your leader will be your advocate, but there will be instances when they won't be. Before requesting help from someone else, have a conversation with that person. Let them know what you hope to achieve and how they can help. Not everyone is willing and able to play this role; don't be disappointed if you get rejected. Better to know upfront than to get a half-hearted commitment.

There are other circumstances in which you unexpectedly find an advocate. A leader may notice your potential or strong performance and take the initiative to become your advocate.

Regardless of how the relationship begins, don't squander the opportunity to be coached by an experienced leader. An advocate plays an important role, and their insights will be instrumental in your development. Once you have an advocate, establish clear expectations. Discuss the type of engagement that will best fit your situation. For example, decide whether you are looking for informal or structured guidance.

Advocacy and development go hand in hand. Some companies emphasize a formal feedback process, while other firms use an informal, as-needed format. Regardless of the company's culture, your development plan should take into account feedback from an advocate. Incorporate this information into year-end and mid-year reviews—this will help you to focus on specific development areas. Figure 5 illustrates a comprehensive development plan and its components.

Let's discuss development and the tools that you can leverage. The building blocks of a comprehensive development plan are assessment tools (such as the Myers-Briggs Type Indicator and DiSC Assessment), mid-year reviews, year-end reviews, and, in some cases, 360-degree surveys. Your leader's feedback should be consistent throughout. If you get a year-end review that highlights meeting deadlines as a gap in your performance, you should expect the same feedback in other types of reviews. In addition, your development plan should include specific actions you can take to close these gaps.

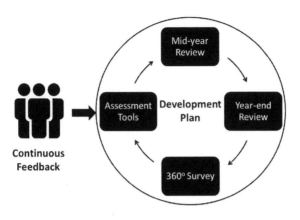

Figure 5 – Development Plan

While 360-degree surveys aren't typically used, when they are, they can give you important insights not generally found in a year-end or mid-year review. In a 360-degree survey, your leader, peers, and people who report to you are all asked to provide feedback on your strengths and weaknesses. This can be a very useful source of information. It is not uncommon to see differences across groups, because each group's feedback is based on a different perspective. Given your unique relationship with your leader, their opinion may be very different from those of your peers or direct reports.

You should focus on the areas where you see similar feedback from all groups. If there are points of divergence, then take stock of each one. Determine with your leader (or advocate) the most immediate areas to focus on. Concentrate on those that will generate the biggest benefits. Keep all other areas that were identified (but not a priority) on your action plan for future consideration. The development planning process is an evolving one that never really ends; the areas of focus will change over time.

Another component of a development plan is assessment tools such as the Myers-Briggs Type Indicator (MBTI). MBTI is a psychological self-assessment questionnaire that provides insights into how individuals make decisions and perceive their environments. Having gone through this evaluation a number of times over the years, I've found it provides both helpful insights and consistent conclusions. It also provides useful information about how people process information, communicate, and respond to others. Integration of the Myers-Briggs assessment into your development plan will provide a valuable perspective and complement the feedback you receive.

Human resources (HR) teams are the corporate guardians of development plans, and they typically provide the support and tools your firm utilizes. Unfortunately, the importance placed on employee development sometimes turns out to be more lip service than substance. Compounding this is the possibility that HR is underutilized, not up to the task, or treated as an extraneous support function. If development plans and processes are low priorities at your company, it could signal that mangers are simply "checking off the box" in their evaluations. If this is the case, don't despair. You can design your own development plan. Follow these steps:

- Identify one person—or a few people—willing to help you. If you're working with a group, give them the option to keep their feedback anonymous. In any case, make it clear that you intend to take action in response to the feedback.

- Create a form for them to fill out. Having a standard form is important to maintain consistency. Ask for general observations, strengths, development areas, and recommendations. You can also include a "Start, Stop, Continue" section. This asks those giving feedback what you should start to do, stop doing, and continue to do.

- Review the feedback you received and summarize the findings. Share the feedback with those that provided it. Include the top priorities you will commit to working on.

- Schedule updates periodically to assess progress and adjust as needed.

Many factors will contribute to your success, but having an advocate can be invaluable to your development and career advancement. If you're lucky enough to find an advocate, keep in mind that it requires a commitment on your part to manage your plan and nurture this relationship. Some advocates will proactively coach you, but most will seek your active participation. Advocates can disconnect if you give them a reason. For example, if you don't commit to the development process, start to slip on deliverables, don't meet deadlines, or come up short on specific goals, the tide of support can turn against you.

What makes for effective coaching will depend on your specific situation, and you'll need to decide what options work best for you. Once you have an action plan, set clear goals and objectives with timelines that include periodic reviews. The right advocate(s) will help you to review feedback, prioritize your opportunities, and stay focused on achieving success.

"After about three lessons the voice teacher said, 'Don't take voice lessons. Do it your way.'"

—Johnny Cash

---

෨ ෫

Chapter 13

MAKE IT A PRIORITY TO MENTOR AND BECOME AN ADVOCATE FOR OTHERS.

"Tell me and I forget; teach me and I may remember; involve me and I will learn."

—*Dr. Herb True*

THE PREVIOUS CHAPTER discussed in depth how advocacy and mentoring can be essential to your self-improvement. It is important to get help; it is equally important to become an advocate for others. The support you provide can range from helpful day-to-day pointers to more structured mentoring. You can give guidance to just about anyone: a friend, a family member, a peer, or even a leader.

If you take a moment to think about those who've had an influence on you, can you recall what specifically made a difference? Was it sound advice? A new insight? Did they help you through a rough spot?

When advising others, use the same processes that helped you.

You can be a mentor or advocate at any level, but you'll find yourself in this role more often the higher as you move up in an organization. As you gain experience and build a reputation as a leader, others will proactively turn to you for guidance. Be careful not to overcommit and take on too many mentees, as it will dilute your effectiveness. Understand the amount of time and level of engagement you will need for working with a mentee, and carve out the appropriate time on your calendar.

As a mentor, you take on a role of a trusted advisor. People depend on you to provide honest, candid feedback. It's a commitment you need to take seriously. Assure them that conversations will be keep confidential. Remember how important your advocates were to you when you were the one getting advice. If you are unwilling to make the commitment, it is best to respectfully decline and recommend another person.

A relationship with a mentee will vary depending on whether they are motivated and committed or were coerced into working with you. When possible, avoid people who are being pressured to work with a mentor, as they will generally be resistant or not committed to the process. Your reputation could be tarnished if your mentee falls short of meeting expectations.

Even those who are motivated may be uncomfortable getting constructive feedback or may misconstrue it as criticism. Be candid, but be mindful of the tone in which you deliver guidance, especially if you have a different communication style than your mentee. Getting feedback can create stress, so be sure to position your feedback as constructive and share it in a collaborative manner. If your feedback comes across negatively or you convey it in a critical tone, your mentee may become reluctant to commit to the process.

Demonstrate your support and commitment to helping your mentee succeed. Reinforce progress with positive feedback. For example, when a mentee demonstrates that they stepped up and managed a project effectively, tell them that. This approach will reduce stress levels all around, and with it, your mentees are likely to be more open to accepting your advice and committing to a plan.

People will seek out your advice on a range of topics. Be clear on when you can help. If you're not comfortable with a topic or lack the insight for the advice someone seeks, then be honest and refer that person to someone better suited to help them.

Major categories of advice you may be asked to help with are: performance in a role, attaining a new role (either promotion or a lateral move), handling a tough situation, managing a stressful relationship, focusing on specific development areas, transitioning to a new role, and communicating effectively. The format of your advice can range from a one-off conversation to a structured development plan. Each of these formats has a set of unique characteristics; know which one to use in what circumstances. One-off and informal conversations are best used to address topics as they occur, while a formal plan is best suited for longer-term guidance. Use this framework to guide you in creating a formal mentoring plan:

1. Have an initial meeting to discuss the type of advice being sought.

2. Agree on each person's responsibilities and expectations.

3. Decide on focus area(s) and objectives.

4. Determine the engagement model (formal or informal).

5. Craft an action plan with specific steps to address focus area(s).

6. Determine success metrics and create a scorecard to track progress.

7. Schedule time to review feedback provided by others and to validate progress.

The first three steps will help to establish the nature of the relationship and the focus areas. Collaborate in determining the roles and responsibilities of you and your mentee. Will the advice be reactive or proactive? Will you have a structured process or will you provide informal feedback? Customize the frequency and method of feedback based on the needs of the person you are working with. Some people like informal, verbal feedback, while others prefer to get feedback in writing. Understand what works best for your mentee and how to deliver the most effective plan for them.

Once you have clearly established roles and articulated objectives, it is equally important to establish a blueprint for implementation. Without an operating plan that lays out specific steps for what needs to be done, you face the risk of falling short. This plan should include scheduling meetings (and keeping them), speaking with others as needed to gather feedback, and tracking progress against expectations.

Having clear objectives will help you stay on track. Commit to supporting your mentee, and be patient. Remember that they are sorting through issues and may need time to figure out how to move forward. Even though they may be apprehensive, they took an important first step in coming to you.

Take the time to uncover underlying issues or circumstances prior to providing advice. Reinforce feedback through scheduled updates or in real time when you observe specific behaviors. Feedback you provide needs to be actionable and directly related to development areas. When a mentee is responsive to feedback and is committed to change, that's a sign you've earned their trust.

Don't underestimate the value of establishing success metrics; it's much easier to gauge success if you have a target to aim for. Success metrics can be either qualitative or quantitative. Qualitative measures include observations of behavior, presentation style, clarity of communications, etc. Quantitative measures are more tangible; they include improvement in feedback ratings and reaching specific business targets (e.g., sales).

It is possible that you will simultaneously be a mentor and a mentee. Your development doesn't end with the next promotion or new job; it is a continuous process throughout your career. As you go through your own development plans, keep in mind the lessons you've learned, and apply them when you provide guidance to others.

Taking on the role of an advocate and mentor can be one of your most rewarding professional achievements. It will give you a great sense of satisfaction to know you've made a difference in someone's career. That's a legacy well worth pursuing.

"Life's most persistent and urgent question is, 'What are you doing for others?'"

—*Martin Luther King, Jr.*

పు ‿

Chapter 14

BEWARE OF THE DETRACTORS IN YOUR CAREER.

"False friends are worse than bitter enemies."

—*Proverb*

I'VE BEEN FORTUNATE to work for many leaders who were advocates and sponsors. Sometimes their feedback came as a surprise, but their supportive approaches enabled me to make progress and close gaps.

But not all my leaders were interested in my development, and that created a few career speed bumps and detours. It is disappointing and demoralizing when your leader doesn't appear to be committed to helping you. The reasons can vary from having their own challenges with job performance to not being adept at helping others—or simply being unwilling.

Under one leader, I received a less-than-enthusiastic year-end evaluation. This specific year-end review marked a seminal moment in my career. I'd had a good year, met or surpassed most goals, and I was hoping to be recognized for these accomplishments. I did not get that recognition; the review was mediocre and my performance ratings fell far short of the tangible results I'd achieved. My self-appraisal, submitted to my leader for input to my year-end review, was returned without a crease—it hadn't even been read! I respectfully disagreed on the performance ratings, providing unequivocal examples of what I'd achieved. By that time, I knew my ship was taking on water, and I decided to stand up for myself. Then the meeting took an interesting turn.

I took out my 360-degree review and proceeded to highlight the results.

The 360-degree review was an evaluation of core performance areas, with subcategories for each. It included feedback from my leader, peers, people reporting to me, and other senior leaders. Each category was comprised of a series of questions in which respondents ranked me on a numeric scale. One was the lowest rating, indicating poor performance, and ten was the highest rating, indicating exceptional performance.

When I had first gotten my 360-degree review, I'd noticed a stark contrast between my leader's ratings and those of the other groups. The gap between the two was so large I thought my leader had made a mistake when filling out the survey. My direct reports, peers, and other senior leaders had consistently ranked me from eight to ten. But my leader's ranking was lower than all the others in nearly every category. In fact, it was often 40–50 percent below the average score of the other groups.

I proceeded to review these results with my leader, noting the rather large discrepancy across all categories. I had neatly lined up all the categories and rankings for each group side by side, and it was clear how low my leader's scores were. I asked how a broad cross-section of the company could have consistently ranked me higher across the board than my leader had. I emphasized that it wasn't one particular category; it was almost all of them. Clearly, I'd hit the right button—my leader became flustered and couldn't give me any reasonable explanation.

While I had the satisfaction of proving my point, I knew the situation wouldn't change. I walked out of that review knowing it would be my last one at that firm. I'd really enjoyed working at the company, but it was clear I was in a no-win situation. I decided it was time to move on.

It's certainly unpleasant to think you may encounter detractors in your career, but chances are it will happen. A detractor can be defined as someone who unfairly maligns a person or willfully employs tactics to delay or derail their work. They could also be a passive detractor, meaning they won't actively work against you, but they will not support you in any way. A detractor may emerge for a number of reasons: organizational changes, conflicting goals, personality differences, insecurity, or competition for a promotion. They could be a leader, peer, or even someone who reports to you.

Having a leader or senior executive who is a detractor can be extremely stressful; you may feel like you are on the defensive at all times. It's a catch-22. On one hand, you may be unwilling to take risks for fear of failure; on the other, this approach can open you to criticism that you're underperforming.

A peer detractor can turn nearly any situation into a proverbial street fight. You are typically dependent on peers to provide the support you need to reach an objective. Without their partnership, you will not be able to make progress.

A direct report who is a detractor will undermine your team's goals and objectives. However, outright subversion or insubordination can lead to dismissal of that person. Because of this, don't expect them to operate openly; typically they operate in ways that allow them to claim plausible deniability.

Knowing that you may have a detractor and understanding how to respond is essential. Your best defense is to be prepared to deal with this unpleasant possibility.

Detractors are typically stealthy; they don't come out and explicitly announce their attitudes toward you. There is a big difference in the underlying motivation between constructive criticism and sabotaging a person. Factors that can be helpful to detect "a disturbance in the Force" include perception, tone and body language, gut instinct, observed behavior, and (to some extent) what you hear through the grapevine. If there are discrepancies between what you hear and observe, alarm bells should be going off. When confronted with a detractor, treat the situation as a time for reflection, stay focused, and remain on track to achieve your goals.

Detractors can be grouped into several categories as described in Table 3. Each type of detractor has their own challenges, and each can present real obstacles to your performance, reputation, and success. Keep in mind not all of these archetypes are actively working against you. But even the passive ones among them can sidetrack you. There are nuances within each of these categories, and countering each type of detractor requires a different approach.

Archetype	Description and Recommended Approach
Insecure worrier	This is a person who is easily rattled by the fear they will fail. They worry about everything from being recognized to getting promoted. They can be a risk-taker, but if things don't go as planned, they can become apoplectic. They can also be passive-aggressive in their dealings with others. Recommended approach: Communicate frequently and demonstrate how the work being done supports success of the group (and them). Suggest alternative solutions if plans unravel.
Backstabber	It looks like everything's sunshine and rainbows when you're dealing with a backstabber, but stay alert. You can have a seemingly good relationship, but they will try to sabotage you if they get the opportunity—especially if it helps them personally. Recommended approach: Build relationships and gain the trust of others who won't easily be swayed by a backstabber. Back up your work with data and the consensus of others.

Archetype	Description and Recommended Approach
Corporate climber	The corporate climber has one and only one goal: self-promotion. They will try to build an empire and staff it with loyalists. They are in a perpetual contest with their peers to secure the next promotion. They view all competitors as a threat. Recommended approach: Convey the linkage between your work and their success. If you can make that connection, there is a good chance they will be your advocate and bring you with them.
Risk avoider	This is a person who avoids making decisions because they may turn out to be the wrong ones. A risk avoider takes the path of least resistance and won't stick their neck out if the outcome is not certain. They have an aversion to anyone who is a risk-taker or pursues innovative solutions that could derail them. Recommended approach: Recognize that being too innovative will work against you. Build a plan that consists of tactical steps to progress to a desired state. You can alleviate a risk avoider's fears if you pursue your strategy in small, sequential steps.

Archetype	Description and Recommended Approach
Fence-sitter	The fence-sitter will be hesitant when required to make a decision. They may suffer from analysis paralysis and need that "one last piece of information." You'll likely get pushback when trying to get them to make a decision, even if the numbers line up. They need to work on their time frame and will make a decision only after being absolutely sure they are comfortable doing so. Recommended approach: Focus on documenting what you're doing, why you're doing it, and what you expect to accomplish. Validation through research or analysis will support your recommendations and reduce their apprehension.
Not invented here	These people are classic roadblocks dressed in team uniforms. They will not accept most ideas, product concepts, etc. from people not on their team. Regardless of the value you bring to a project or team, you are persona non grata. While they won't explicitly say it, their actions make it obvious you're on the outside looking in. Recommended approach: Enlist the help of this person's team and their trusted partners. Building consensus with them will improve the odds of being able to engage and contribute.

Archetype	Description and Recommended Approach
Insecure narcissist	This is the detractor on steroids. It's all about them. They are manically focused on their career. Anyone else's success is a clear and present threat. They view others' triumphs as their failures—even when it comes to people who report to them. Recommended approach: There is a very high likelihood that you're in a no-win situation. Try your best to be viewed as their advocate, but consider new opportunities.

Table 3 – Detractor Archetypes

Detractors may not be avoidable, but you can take steps to mitigate their impact and work to influence their opinions. In some cases, you can change the mindset of a detractor by building a strong relationship with them or people they trust. Clear communications and division of responsibilities will alleviate confusion and reduce the odds of creating a detractor in the first place. Although there is no bulletproof approach, the following steps will strengthen your defenses and help you weather the storm. Detractors will be quick to undermine you, so be diligent to remove valid reasons for their criticism. Good business practices are a vital hedge to thwart a detractor.

- Document everything. This means that all decisions and discussions are documented and shared among a team. This will affirm any agreements made during meetings and reduce the chance of others claiming that they had a different interpretation. Treat documentation as your survival guide.

- Align to goals. Detractors will be swift to point out that your project is not aligned to the company's goals and should be shut down. Demonstrate that any projects you propose will enhance, not deter, the company's goals. This will provide a clear message to others across the company that the work being done is in complete alignment to corporate objectives.

- Get all requirements. Before proposing a project, gather all short-term and long-term requirements from across functional areas. If you don't fully understand requirements at the initial launch, there is a very real risk that a major rework will be needed down the line. Leaders don't like surprises and will confuse these needed future updates with going beyond the scope of the project. Be explicit when it comes to creating a road map and determining the timing for current and future deliverables.

- Stay focused. When starting a new project, don't boil the ocean. Detractors will be quick to point out when a project has too broad a focus. It is a valid criticism, and detractors will be all too happy to communicate their concerns to others. When introducing a new product or process, create a phased implementation plan. Document each phase of the plan, and have a clearly defined objective, as well as milestones and a measurable outcome (or outcomes).

- Aim for the long term. Projects sometimes fail because the goal is to launch phase one and no consideration is given to subsequent phases. A minimally viable product or experience (MVP/E) is a great way to get to market quickly, but it opens the risk that items placed on a future release list will never be implemented. Detractors will jump on this, especially if a product or service falls short of its intended full-feature version, leaving consumers and coworkers unhappy.

Clearly communicate what is being delivered and when, as well as what is being set aside for future consideration.

If you find yourself in a situation involving a detractor, you'll need patience, fortitude, and a game plan to navigate your way through it. Be aware of indications that you have a detractor, including misalignment between words and actions, being excluded from team meetings, and being ignored or avoided. The best option is to resolve the situation by addressing any preconceived notions that may negatively impact your standing. Focus on staying positive, provide clear and concise communications, build relationships, and keep others looped in, especially when the situation impacts them. Be proactive in rectifying the situation, but recognize that there may be irreconcilable relationships, especially with a detractor.

The silver lining is that each of these situations will help you develop the skills needed to navigate similar circumstances in the future. Keep in mind that as hard as you may try, there may be times your best option is to move on. Although a detractor's opposition can result in a door closing, it will also open doors to new opportunities.

"Dishonesty, cowardice and duplicity are never impulsive."

—George A. Knight

৵ ৶

Chapter 15

A LEADER'S ACTIONS AND WORDS NEED TO BE COMPLETELY ALIGNED.

"Words may show a man's wit, but actions his meaning."

—*Benjamin Franklin*

IN THE COURSE of any career, there will be many opportunities to learn from colleagues and leaders. One of the more memorable moments that has stuck with me was when Ken Chenault, then CEO at American Express, made an observation about leadership. He said, "A leader's words and actions need to be completely aligned."

Consistency between words and actions can make the difference between earning respect and being viewed with cynicism. People who demonstrate this consistency build a reputation for credibility. They're viewed as worthy of respect. Others understand that when they communicate something, they'll follow through.

Consistency also alleviates the angst caused by flip-flopping. It creates a stable environment in which people can focus on their goals without the fear that their leader will suddenly change direction. Trying to hit a moving target is not easy. If people can't be sure what they're aiming for, they'll be inclined to do the minimum.

It's important to establish a personal reputation that when you say you're going to do something, you do it. If you are inconsistent, your credibility will suffer. Additionally, people will be hesitant to collaborate with you because of the uncertainly they feel. This is especially true at higher-level positions. Leaders are expected to set the tone and model behavior for all employees of a company. The best CEOs lead by example.

Hypocrisy in leaders fosters a tainted work culture because it creates inconsistencies between words and behavior. It's hard to respect a person who is a proponent of a specific policy or a type of behavior for others, but not for themselves. Leaders are particularly susceptible to this double standard. Their position of authority allows them to create their own rules, and others may be understandably intimidated to point this out. This behavior tends to undermine morale and sets a precedent that the rules are there for convenience and will be applied unequally.

Strong workplace cultures are based on mutual respect, consistency, and one set of principles that every person adheres to. Cultures that don't follow this paradigm will be less effective and will suffer from higher employee dissatisfaction, lower productivity, and increased turnover. Over time, this will lead to what I call the taxation of inconsistency: the added cost of operating and managing in an environment that is likely to be dysfunctional because priorities are uncertain.

Think about your own experiences and how you felt working for a leader who led by example, who demonstrated consistency between words and actions. On the other side of the spectrum, what did you feel when working with a person whose words and deeds were inconsistent?

These are things you should be mulling over when making a choice between roles and leaders. Naturally, prioritize the options that offer the best likelihood for growth and align with your career aspirations. Once you have considered your priorities and preferences, dig into the leadership and team culture. Don't be afraid to ask questions about the workplace environment, leadership styles, and relationships.

Look for the telltale signs of underlying problems. Ask each interviewer the same question(s), and listen for consistency in their answers. Research online reviews and other third-party sources that may shed some light on what it is like to work for the company. The more research you do up front, the better positioned you will be to make the right career choice.

We've discussed aspects of consistency between words and actions as they relate to others, but what does this mean for you? You must make a deliberate and conscious effort to be aware of your own behavior. Avoid being inconsistent in your words and actions, even unintentionally. Are you respectful and courteous to superiors but impatient and dismissive to peers or to your team members? Has a leader or a coworker identified a situation when you've been inconsistent in your words and actions? Is this a subject that's come up in a year-end review, employee feedback, or some other development discussion?

Ask yourself these questions on a regular basis. Consistency between your actions and words is an important way to bolster your personal reputation (your brand) among your coworkers. This alone will not guarantee success, but it is an essential ingredient. When you establish a reputation for doing what you say you will, people will notice, respect you, and want to work with you.

"A leader is one who knows the way, goes the way, and shows the way."

—*John C. Maxwell*

ॐ ॐ

Chapter 16

EMULATE THE LEADERS YOU MOST ADMIRE AND RESPECT.

"Leadership is hard to define and good leadership even harder. But if you can get people to follow you to the ends of the earth, you are a great leader."

—*Indra Nooyi*

WHAT MAKES A leader great can vary significantly; there is no single blueprint for success. The characteristics and tactics of one leader may not necessarily work for another leader. One company I worked for had a CEO who was a tough-minded analytical thinker; the company's president, on the other hand, was a visionary and a charismatic communicator. Together, their skills complemented one another, and that made them stronger as a team. Both individuals were successful, yet it would have been impossible for them to swap these qualities and enjoy the same levels of success.

The reason? It is very difficult to excel in an area that you are not well suited for. For example, you may want to be a visionary, but unless you have that natural inclination, you will struggle or fail. Maybe your strength is in analytics and numbers. Trying to apply these skills to playing the role of a big thinker could backfire. Visionaries don't necessarily rely on numbers; they have a keen understanding of trends, as well as the blue-sky thinking necessary for ideation. An analytical mind would likely rely on numbers and projections, which could get in the way of brainstorming.

So what are your strengths? How do you know what they are? It may be difficult to delineate between your strongest skills and the ones you desire, but don't possess. Two ways to tell what you're actually good at are listening to the feedback of others and looking at where your performance consistently meets or exceeds expectations. Conversely, negative feedback, low performance, or difficulty in certain areas should be a sign they are not your strong suits. Chances are, this won't change. But that should not discourage you from working at turning a weakness into a strength. Training and experience can turn things around. Be realistic about what is possible to improve and what isn't.

Your development should be predicated on finding the qualities that are the best fit for you; this will be a key ingredient in your effectiveness as a leader. Know your strengths and weaknesses. Focus on what you're good at and understand where there is room for improvement. Sometimes it may not be possible to improve on a weakness. This may be due to a lack of skill—or desire—to remediate it.

It's okay to have weak points; you're human, after all. Don't ignore them; find solutions that will help you close gaps. Smart leaders hire others who have skills or expertise that they lack. For example, if you're not good at marketing, hire someone who is. Leaders who are intimidated by the thought of relying on others to fill in their own gaps create the same blind spots on their team.

When you come across someone you admire and respect, dig deeper into what attributes are influencing your opinion. Are they supportive, smart, trustworthy, or funny? Pay attention to body language, facial expressions, and tone as you assess the overall demeanor of a person. You can learn a lot from observation, and you'll pick up on certain attributes you like and others you don't.

Over time, you will likely internalize and adopt the visual and verbal cues you wish to emulate. It's a worthwhile investment of your time to understand and interpret leadership qualities and consider how they can help you in your own growth plans. This process is a confluence of art and science; you'll be touching on the psychology of leadership as you pursue an understanding of those attributes you admire most or least.

While the list below is not exhaustive, it's a good representation of leadership attributes you can focus on. Start with some of the more basic attributes, especially early in your career. These include communication, empathy, focus, honesty, and passion. You can hone your skills in these areas regardless of your experience. As you take on larger roles and begin to manage others, attributes such as empowerment, accountability, tenacity, and decisiveness will become more important.

Keep in mind that you shouldn't try to master every attribute on this list. Instead, focus on those qualities that you find most desirable and best suited to you. Be realistic when assessing the list, and keep in mind the distinction between what is desirable versus what is reasonable. Once you hone the list to a select few attributes, you can incorporate them into a learning or development plan.

- Accountability – Take responsibility for your actions regardless of whether they work out or not.

- Authentic – What you see is what you get; no surprises.

- Courage – Be brave and voice your opinion; take chances; embrace innovation.

- Compassion – Understand people may fail; provide support to help others succeed.

- Communication – Whether in verbal or written form, be clear, concise, and consistent.

- Confidence – Have conviction in your decisions even through difficult periods.

- Decisiveness – Utilize the information needed to make a decision, but don't overanalyze.

- Emotional intelligence – Manage relationships based on individual personalities; understand how to engage and communicate effectively with others.

- Empathy – Put yourself in others' shoes before rushing to judge them.

- Empowerment – Equip others to achieve the unexpected; give them the support and tools they need to get the job done.

- Focus – Concentrate on your objectives and what you need to do to reach them.

- Honesty – Be candid when dealing with others; be honest with yourself about who you are.

- Inspiration – Motivate others; embrace innovation; help others achieve what they thought was impossible.

- Open-mindedness – Consider others' opinions and thoughts; embrace diversity of opinion.

- Passion – Care intensely about what you do—but don't let your enthusiasm get in the way of sound decision-making.

- Perseverance – Expunge the word "quit" from your vocabulary; know the difference between quitting and reaching an end point.

- Toughness – Develop the fortitude to take on the challenges that stand in the way of delivering results—even when it isn't popular.

Focus on the attributes that play to your strengths, and coworkers will see you as being genuine. They will be more willing to work with you. People who can motivate others, build trust, or go to great lengths to support their team will gain a following.

Leaders like Richard Branson, Mary Barra, Marc Benioff, Oprah Winfrey, and Mark Zuckerberg are the corporate equivalent of rock stars to their employees. They are part of an elite group that broke the mold—a group of legendary business icons who obtained cult-like followings and loyalty. These types of leaders are charismatic and know how to motivate people to achieve a common goal.

In contrast to domineering leaders, they build camaraderie and foster a sense of common purpose. Authoritative leaders' unrelenting focus can have a detrimental effect on their coworkers, despite their success. Consensus-building leaders set the strategy and tone for a business, but they know they can't do it alone. It's the reason they're so good at defining their visions and bringing others with them on the journey. They are quick to recognize the efforts of their teams and celebrate their wins. They work toward a goal, stay on course, and don't give up easily—but they also know when to throw in the towel. These types of leaders don't look back; rather they navigate the course they have charted.

Regardless of your level, initially focus on developing your base skills. As you ascend the organizational ladder, the leadership skills you require will vary. The attributes that were helpful in getting you to your current level may not be the same ones you'll need at the next level. Over time, your focus will shift to reflect a greater emphasis on leadership and mentoring.

It's a good idea to continuously identify and monitor those attributes you admire in leaders or others whom you respect. Incorporate them into your training programs or development plan. You will not be strong in all areas, so don't try to be superhuman. Focus on your strengths, and use them to achieve your goals. Be comfortable in your own skin, and success will come to you.

"I am the greatest. I said that even before I knew I was."

—*Muhammad Ali*

Chapter 17

IF YOUR LEADER DOESN'T SUPPORT YOUR DEVELOPMENT, ASSESS YOUR OPTIONS.

"Life is change. Growth is optional. Choose wisely."

—*Karen Kaiser Clark*

To COIN A variation of a classic *Forrest Gump* line, leaders are like a box of chocolates; you never know what you'll get. I will reiterate throughout this book that you are ultimately responsible for your development—but you can't do it all alone. You need the guidance and experience of one or more leaders.

I learned a saying during my time at Monster Worldwide: "People don't quit companies; they quit bosses." There are several reasons someone might take the drastic step of quitting because of a boss. One is an absence of the desirable leadership attributes discussed in

Chapters 15 and 16. You may come across a leader who is impatient, doesn't empathize, has a do-as-I-say-and-not-as-I-do mentality, or creates a toxic work environment.

No leader is perfect; they each have their pros and cons. Some are incredibly supportive in providing development opportunities, while others don't make it a priority.

Sometimes, a leader is so unsupportive it crosses a red line: a point beyond which change is inevitable. You may have the option to trudge on in a less-than-perfect situation until you find something better. But waiting too long can be risky because the lack of support may indicate that you are not in the boss's long-term plans. Would you know if that's the case? It may be difficult to be sure. If your leader is more focused on their career development than yours, they may simply be passively unsupportive. On the other hand, if a leader is more critical of you than others or bypasses you for new opportunities, it's something more ominous. In either case, your growth will stagnate. Reaching this point means that you have to make some important choices regarding not whether to move on, but when.

This doesn't mean you should pack your bags and quit your job at the first sign of trouble. You should keep things in perspective. Remember that the grass is always greener on the other side of the fence... until you jump over to the other side. You'll likely trade one set of challenges for another; they may be better or worse, but you won't know for certain until you transition. Don't be too hasty to move to a different group or a new company unless you've hit the proverbial wall. Examine your options carefully. If you decide that moving on is the your only option, map out your goals and timeframe. Patience and research will be your best allies as you plot out a new course.

Let's discuss some rules of engagement. It's important to get the facts that will drive a decision to move on. Start by asking questions such as: Is my leader willing to support my development? Will they invest the time needed to make progress? Get answers to these questions. Sit down with your leader and have a candid discussion on your goals and what you expect from them.

Another consideration is whether your leader has the will and the skill to actively participate in creating and supporting your development plan. Both attributes are important, and a leader who lacks one of them can hamstring your development. Having a leader with the skill but not the will results in a half-hearted process that will lead to a suboptimal plan. A leader with the will but not the skill, on the other hand, may be committed but unable to pull together an effective plan. Ideally you want a leader ready, willing, and able to help you.

Remember to carefully evaluate the options available to you prior to taking action. If your leader is unsupportive and not giving you appropriate feedback or guidance, then change sooner rather than later is appropriate.

After you have done your due diligence, it's time to make a choice. If you are comfortable with your leader's commitment and believe you will have the support you need, great. If you believe that your immediate leader is not up to the task, find a proxy or move on, either to a new group or to a new company.

Changing roles can be rewarding and recharge your career. But beware of the pitfalls and mistakes that can occur in a transition.

You may be allured by a fancy title or compensation rather than the merits of the role. Or you may be tempted to move to a "hot" company… but maybe its culture isn't a good fit for you.

You can reduce these risks by doing your homework: make sure you understand your new job description and the corporate culture. Seek out connections within your network—people who work or know others at your target firm. Ask them about the culture, team, and leadership of the company. Leverage business social networks that can provide additional feedback and insights.

There are also a variety of resources that provide information on public companies, including annual reports or other company documents, brokerage company research, etc. They'll give you useful information on financial performance over the short and long term. This research will help you find those firms that offer the best opportunity for growth. There is no guarantee that you'll have all the answers you need, but doing your due diligence will increase the likelihood of having the information you need for a successful transition.

Start with a checklist that details the key tasks needed for a transition plan. Determine your professional goals, including the type of job you want and whether you want to make a lateral move or aim for a more senior role. Focus on the roles that are of the greatest interest to you and the companies you most want to work for. Do your research, though in some cases, not all the information you seek will be available. Use the following checklist:

Factor	Considerations
Role	Can you stay in your current role? How long do you want to remain in your current position? Are you looking for a promotion or lateral move? Do you want a position in the same functional discipline?
Career path	What potential roles fit into your long-term career path? Will the role you are considering help you get to the next level? What skills are you looking to build?
Leader	What is the reputation of your prospective leader? Are they known to develop their team members based on meritocracy or favoritism?
Compensation	Are you willing to take a pay cut? What is your target salary and bonus? What health insurance and other benefits does your target firm offer? Do the vacation and time-off allowances meet your needs?
Company	Do you want to stay at your current firm? Are you interested in working for a competitor? Do you want to stay in the same industry? How is the company performing? What is its reputation as an employer? What is the feedback on social media from current employees?
Culture	Is the culture a good fit for your work style? Are current employees satisfied with the leadership? Do you believe that the company embraces a work-life balance? Do they sponsor charities or other causes you are passionate about?

Factor	Considerations
Location	Where do you want to work? What is your ideal commute time? Are you willing to relocate to another city or country?

The best course of action may not be obvious. Weigh the trade-offs involved in changing departments within a firm or jumping ship to a different company. At the top of the list should be your likelihood of making a successful transition to a new position or company. A transition within a company usually removes several unknowns that come with joining a new firm. But do keep in mind that business groups within a company, especially a large firm, can vary in terms of culture and leadership.

Whether a move within your company is possible will depend in part on the relationship you have with your leader, their reputation and influence, and the size of the company. If your leader is simply unwilling to invest the time in your development, it may make sense to look elsewhere within the company. If your leader is a detractor and they are respected or influential, your options will be limited, as others may be reluctant to bring you onto their teams. Of course, this will largely depend on your leader's relationship with others; if it is acrimonious, it may actually make a move easier.

Not all job changes occur because you've hit an impasse; they can also come from new growth opportunities. You could receive new offers from within your company or from another firm. In either situation, having a transition plan will help you as you move to a new role. A move within a company is less complicated—you know the company, its culture, and likely, the leader and their team. Moving to a new company, whether by choice or necessity, will require a more comprehensive transition plan. The good news is that you're employed and earning an income; therefore, you have the luxury of planning for a transition.

Finding the right fit with respect to both a new position and a new company will take time, even in a strong job market. Determine whether each prospective role offers the opportunity for upward mobility over time. Choose options that put you on a desirable career trajectory—one that includes personal development and growth.

Don't underestimate the role a leader plays in your career development. Even a bad leader can be a role model—of what not to do. However, if they aren't committed, it's time to move on. A leader or an influencer who is committed to your personal growth will have a lasting positive impact on your career.

Remember this, and pay it back when you're in the boss's chair.

"You do not lead by hitting people over the head. Any damn fool can do that, but it's usually called 'assault'—not 'leadership.'"

—*Dwight D. Eisenhower*

Chapter 18

GET IT IN WRITING OR ASSUME IT WON'T HAPPEN.

"Every organization of men, be it social or political, ultimately relies on man's capacity for making promises and keeping them."

—Hannah Arendt

I PROMISE, I guarantee it, it's a lock, don't worry, trust me—if you've heard any of these declarations, then you've likely learned the hard way how hollow they can be. Without written confirmation, you have no guarantees, and if someone fails to follow through, you'll have no recourse. Should you find yourself in a situation where someone uses one of these verbal "promises," alarm bells should go off. And if that person refuses to put their promise in writing, that should amplify the sound level. People don't usually make promises they don't plan on keeping, but it happens. It's up to you to gauge the credibility of the person making the commitment. The Latin phrase *caveat emptor* comes to mind. It translates as "let the buyer beware."

"Your word is everything," sounds old-fashioned, but back in the old days, your word and a handshake sealed a deal. It's hard to believe, in our modern world of contracts and litigation, that a simple verbal agreement and handshake were once enough to conduct commerce. Today we recognize that without a concrete, written agreement, one should not be surprised if a promise is not kept.

Knowing the person making the promise and their track record of keeping their word can reduce your risk. But there will be circumstances when events render someone's ability to deliver on a promise or expectation impossible. Change is a constant that can't be completely planned for, and it can have an impact on the agreements you have with others.

Once, early on in my career, a leader told me a promotion was imminent. He had been promoted and I was being tapped to take his former role. I was thrilled. It was a big step for me. This happened on a Friday. When I came into work on Monday, my leader backtracked and said that I wasn't ready for the promotion, but maybe "next time" it could happen. It was devastating.

When I pushed back, he tried to convince me I had mistaken his intention. I wasn't the most assertive person, but to my credit, I stood up for myself. I kept my cool but stuck to my guns and articulated my case as best I could. I told him that he unequivocally assured me I was to be promoted, and by backtracking he made it seem that any prospect of a future promotion was a distant hope at best. For me, it was a now-or-never moment.

After a lengthy discussion, my leader relented and reluctantly admitted that he had indeed made a promise to me regarding the promotion. Although he said he wouldn't go back on his word, he also said I wasn't fully ready for the role. The message I got was, "You're on your own and I won't save you if you sink." It was a disappointing way to start a promotion. If this was the kickoff to a more senior role, what could I expect when I ran into the normal array of corporate challenges and obstacles? I was confident that I would work hard and be successful, but having only half-hearted support was tough to accept.

My leader's boss also expressed doubts about my abilities. He had been tapped for a new role in a different business group and my leader had been promoted into his role. During a meeting with me, he mentioned that he'd heard about the promotion. He told me that in his honest opinion, I wasn't ready, but he thought in time I would be. His less-than-enthusiastic assessment of my readiness was a disappointment. I clearly remember my response to him. I said, "Please keep that bar low, and I'll be even more impressive when I succeed."

I was motivated to prove him wrong. I worked relentlessly and learned much in the new role. Most importantly, I exceeded the expectations of my leader's former boss, and about eighteen months later, he offered me a newly created role in his business unit.

This episode left an indelible mark on me. I'd nearly lost an opportunity that was promised to me, one that turned into an important stepping-stone in my career. Prior to this episode, I'd assumed that a verbal promise was an absolute guarantee.

There were two important lessons I took away from this situation. First, you need to push back (respectfully) when someone tries to renege on a promise. Sometimes this works; however, know when it becomes counterproductive and you need to let go. Second, and more importantly, I learned that I couldn't count on a promise. As a consequence, I am very cynical when someone is not willing to put a commitment in writing. In fact, I'm not willing to make any verbal promises in business—or even make a suggestion of a verbal promise. I may convey what my intentions are, but there is a very big difference between stating what I hope to do for someone and promising to do it.

To mitigate the risks associated with a broken promise, be diligent in turning verbal assurances into written ones when possible. Without the proper approvals, getting any type of promise in writing will be a challenge. Any good company's legal or human resource representative will vehemently advise against even a suggestion of a promise. These groups are responsible for protecting the company from litigation or reputational risk. Unless something is a certainty, they advise never putting promises in writing.

If someone makes you a promise, ensure that you document everything that relates to it, such as meetings and agreed upon performance goals. If possible, use email as a way to confirm what was said or shared during meetings. Even without a written promise, it will be much easier to close the deal with supporting documentation. It will also be more difficult for someone to walk back a promise. Verbal promises without corroborating evidence will be difficult, if not impossible, to enforce.

In some circumstances, getting a written commitment, or contract, is not only usual; it is required. Examples include project deliverables, letters of intent, job offers, statements of work, etc. Not many of us would accept a job offer without having specific details of compensation and responsibilities in writing. Negotiating contracts can be a tedious and complex task. A good contract outlines the details of what is expected by each party, including specific tasks, deliverables, timeframes, costs, and accountability measures. It also lays out the consequences if a party fails to deliver on these commitments.

There are other situations in which getting a commitment in writing is not typical and may even be awkward. For instance, when seeking initial estimates in the early stage of a project, don't expect to get any guarantees. An estimate is just that, an educated guess. Working out actual figures requires due diligence, and you should expect them only at a later stage (but prior to signing a contract).

When the roles are reversed and you're the one making promises, make sure that you do your homework and understand what you are committing to. You shouldn't make a commitment unless you are absolutely sure you can deliver on it. This is more critical when the stakes are high and reneging on a promise has consequences. Missing a meeting could annoy others, but not meeting contractual obligations will have more serious ramifications. In many cases, it's typical to get approval from your leader before committing to deliverables.

If someone verbally makes you a promise, do yourself a favor and get it in writing. If they're unwilling to take that step, then don't get your hopes up.

"Vote for the man who promises least; he'll be the least disappointing."

—*Bernard Baruch*

ഏ ഛ

Chapter 19

INVEST IN YOURSELF; YOU ARE ACCOUNTABLE FOR YOUR DEVELOPMENT.

"Learning never exhausts the mind."

—*Leonardo da Vinci*

There are very few absolute statements one can make about their career development. One you can rely on is this: You need to own your development, period! Continuous improvement and development should be a top priority throughout your career.

In a time-starved work culture, focusing on self-improvement often falls to the bottom of people's to-do lists. We're all caught up in a myriad of meetings, town halls, and one-on-ones, along with an avalanche of daily emails and text messages. While most of us are interested in focusing on personal development, we tend to do it in an unproductive manner.

Start with a process to ascertain specific development areas you need to focus on, and then develop a plan to address them. Keep in mind that you alone are responsible for your development. If you don't make it a priority, no one else will.

A proactive leader will be able to provide significant support and help you chart your course. If you don't believe that you are getting the level of feedback or support necessary to hone your skills, take control of the process. Seek out pertinent information, and craft a plan to address the development areas others identify. Get a robust perspective by including your leader, peers, and people who work for you. Be sure to document what you learn and share it with your leader. Actively manage the process and ask for their feedback and recommendations. Regardless of the situation, make sure you've identified the highest priority areas you need to work on and have a well-documented plan to address them.

There are three sources of feedback that you should consider when developing your plan: your leader, your peers, and, when managing others, your subordinates. The feedback from these groups will form the basis of your development plan. Keep in mind that gathering feedback is a continuous process. You will get some through structured interactions such as year-end or peer reviews. It is also important to seek out informal feedback from others. Regular updates or lunch meetings are some of the settings where you can get this done.

Begin with your leader. They have first-hand experience in working with you, and they are responsible for evaluating your performance and providing feedback. A leader may also seek the opinions of others who work with you or are managed by you. Your leader's feedback will help you to identify and prioritize the more salient areas of your plan.

The second group to seek insight and feedback from is your peers. Colleagues are often an underutilized source, and they will offer you an important perspective, as they can provide observations without the power dynamic that exists between a leader and their direct reports. In addition, this group interacts with you on a day-to-day basis. They will have specific feedback based on interactions with you on projects, in meetings, or in conversations and emails. Company resources that you can use to gather information include 360-degree surveys, mid-year or year-end reviews, and self-assessment tools. Some of these will be mandatory parts of the company's feedback process, while others may be options available to you.

In addition to drawing on company resources, take the initiative to do things on your own. Set up informal conversations with coworkers to discuss their opinions about the areas you can focus on. In order to get a broader perspective, include others from functional areas that you interact with. This might include coworkers who are part of a project team or partners in the finance, legal, or human resources department. These individuals can provide a fresh perspective on what they view as your development opportunities.

The third source you should seek feedback from is your direct reports or others who work under your leadership. This group will present a challenge: namely, it will be more difficult to get candid feedback from them due to their fear of repercussions. They may also worry that you'll be dismissive of their perspectives, be unresponsive to their feedback, or hold a grudge against them. This is the main reason why the anonymous 360-degree feedback process is the best way to get unfiltered, useful information. If your company doesn't offer 360-degree feedback, it may be difficult to get candid feedback. Consider engaging your leader or human resources department to ask for anonymous information from your team. If you choose this path, make sure that you create a standard form for them to fill out. Include an assurance that the process is anonymous, and make it optional.

Good leaders accept feedback with an open mind. You should always follow up by expressing appreciation for the time and contributions provided by others. Let them know you are committed to internalizing the feedback and will create an action plan. Also let your direct reports know that while you might not be able to focus on all areas of feedback, they've been noted. The better the quality of candid, unbiased input, the better chance you'll have of creating a development plan focused on the right areas.

Each of these groups—leaders, peers, and direct reports—provides a unique perspective, and collectively they will contribute to a sound development plan. Keep in mind that each group will have a particular perspective. For example, you might find that your team feels you have strong communications skills, but your leader highlights this as an area for development. This disparity doesn't mean that you can't rely on the feedback or that you must choose one group's input and ignore the rest. If you receive conflicting feedback, your leader's perspective should take precedence. This doesn't mean that the other feedback is less accurate, but your leader is ultimately responsible for your development and performance. Failing to address their concerns could adversely impact your year-end ratings and compensation.

Despite this, you may be able to address differing feedback. Focus on the feedback in the context of who is providing it. Let's go back to the earlier example of your leader who has identified communications as a focus area. Perhaps your leader's feedback refers to communicating more effectively with their peers. At this level, skilled, clear, and concise communication is expected. Should you be unable to raise the bar with this group, it could dampen their perception of you. And if you don't have their confidence, they may be reluctant to support a promotion or expansion of responsibilities. Working on your communications with this group should be a high priority.

So how does this impact the feedback you received from your team? Prioritizing your leader's feedback should not prevent you from responding to the area(s) that your team identified. For example, perhaps your team expressed that they felt a need for more training. Discussing this with your team members will help you to pinpoint the skills they want to improve. You could arrange to have team members to take classes or bring in an expert to hold sessions for the entire team.

Don't ignore feedback; always acknowledge it. Focus on the most pressing needs, but remember that doesn't preclude addressing additional feedback. Should you be faced with too much feedback, start with the highest priorities and, over time, work your way down the list. Be proactive; when you conquer one area, start on the next one.

Learning and development are continuous and conscious processes. Actively manage your development and growth opportunities; be persistent in dedicating effort and time to creating an ongoing plan to drive self-improvement. One of the first things a financial advisor recommends to a new client is that they establish a diversified portfolio of stocks, bonds, etc. Similarly, a development plan must be based on a diverse set of sources and tools to ensure your success.

Ask the people around you for input, and learn what resources are available to you. Find the right combination of trainings, classes, networking, continuing education, conferences, and self-assessment tools to aid you in your growth.

With every new level you ascend to, your focus area(s) will change. You'll eventually master the development areas you're working on today, and new ones will surface.

Don't confuse momentum for success when it comes to your development. While there will be leaders, advocates, or mentors willing to help along the way, it is up to you to ensure that you actively make progress. You are the navigator and explorer who must find new horizons and carve the path forward in your professional life. If you're not satisfied with the road you're on, then carefully plan out the actions you need to take to course correct and get back on track. Make it a priority each year to set targets and goals, and perform self-assessments on a regular basis. This will pay off in personal growth and success throughout your career.

"The purpose of learning is growth, and our minds, unlike our bodies, can continue growing as we continue to live."

—*Mortimer J. Adler*

Chapter 20

BEING CANDID IS IMPORTANT, ESPECIALLY WHEN GIVING CONSTRUCTIVE FEEDBACK.

"Candor is the brightest gem of criticism."
—*Benjamin Disraeli*

BEING HONEST WITH others is a hallmark of a strong leader. It's far easier and more convenient to candy-coat constructive criticism—or avoid it entirely. By nature, most of us are averse to delivering a candid opinion that highlights a shortcoming. Although constructive feedback is aimed at identifying and addressing specific issues, it can be misconstrued by the recipient as something more ominous. These concerns are not restricted to people who report to you; they can also apply to peers or your leader. To reduce this possibility, always be clear from the start that the purpose of your feedback is to help the person receiving it.

There was a time when I did not like to give critical feedback. It made me nervous, and I didn't want to hurt anyone's feelings. Typically my feedback would focus on what a person did well, and I would only lightly touch upon areas for improvement. That changed after I got feedback from my boss. He told me that that being "nice" and not telling someone about a weakness was not helping that person. He said that no one could improve on a weakness if I did not point it out and the performance of my team would suffer as a result. I took his advice and put it into practice. Most people genuinely appreciated my being candid with them and felt it helped them to address development areas.

You have two objectives when giving feedback. First, to raise awareness about an area that needs to be addressed. Second, to provide tangible information that can be used to create specific steps for remediation. The feedback should always be constructive, not destructive.

Because responses to feedback can range from acceptance to defensiveness, be prepared to deal with each. Even when a person accepts feedback, you should follow up to ensure they are taking steps to address the areas you identified. Defensiveness will present a greater challenge, as it indicates reluctance to accept feedback. It is typically accompanied by denial and resistance to any help or guidance. It is very important in these situations to be careful about how you communicate and what you say.

How you deliver feedback is critical how someone responds. Start with the person's strengths, rather than focusing exclusively on development areas. This will balance the discussion and make the recipient more likely to accept the feedback. Show empathy and support. Provide specific examples to support your observations. Rambling on about a shortcoming in general terms will be counterproductive.

For example, if you tell a person they're a poor communicator but don't provide context, you'll come off as disingenuous. Instead, share a specific situation in which they didn't communicate clearly. Let them know what they could have done differently. Always provide an observation and a solution.

Feedback should also demonstrate how a change in behavior can lead to a desired outcome. For example, if the problem was a missed deadline, explain how it impacted a project or eroded the confidence others had in that person to get the job done. List some benefits that would result if that person were to convey that a delay was imminent. First, others would be able to reset their expectations and communicate the impact to their respective teams. Second, senior leaders would know about the delay and the underlying reason(s). It might be a disappointment, but they would understand; it is not uncommon to hit a speed bump. Explain that most leaders become irritated when caught by surprise. Informing them as soon as the delay happens affords them the opportunity to respond.

If there are multiple areas in which you'd like to see improvement, focus on the ones that need immediate attention and hold off on the rest.

Keep in mind that your goal is to help the person you're working with understand and internalize the feedback. Don't only share your thoughts; allow the other person to offer their perspective. Ask them to provide potential solutions and actions they could take to remedy the situation. Don't focus on "what you should do"—instead, make it "what we can do together." Only then will they be able to create a meaningful plan and take corrective action.

Increase the likelihood that your feedback will be effective by following these steps:

1. **Determine focus area(s).** Do your research. Ask others for feedback. Use both personal observations and what you've heard from others.

2. **Set up an initial meeting.** Have a discussion based on your observations or those of others. Suggest area(s) you want to discuss and explain why. Confirm that the person you're working with agrees these are the right areas.

3. **Reference observed behavior.** Describe specific instances that you or others observed that corroborate the feedback. Allow the person you're helping to respond to this feedback. Look for common areas where you agree.

4. **Focus on solutions.** Collaborate on recommendations to address development areas. Include mentoring, training, etc. as options to address top priorities. Share what success would look like.

5. **Review progress.** Get updates from anyone who gave you feedback about the person you're working with. Meet periodically to share feedback and review progress.

There are three major factors that can derail your success when giving feedback—lack of corroboration, no action plan, and lack of ongoing support.

Providing substantiated feedback is a very important first step, but you'll fall short of the goal if you don't have a plan of action. I've witnessed many situations in which a leader provided a perspective to improve specific area(s) but lacked a plan. Another reason why feedback fails is a lack of ongoing support and participation by a leader.

Create a development plan with key milestones to map the progress you expect to see. Success metrics will provide a clear gauge of how the plan is progressing. Figure 6 is a template for a development plan that includes these elements.

Development Plan				
Development Area	Expected Outcome	Action	Success Metric	Deadline
Task 1				
Task 2				

Figure 6 – Development Plan Template

You should monitor and review progress during follow-up discussions. Be respectful but frank during these meetings. Equally important, be sure to recognize any progress or positive movement as it happens.

When is the most appropriate time to provide feedback? The simple answer is always. However, there are different forms of feedback that are appropriate at specific times. These include immediate, in-the-moment opportunities, as well as formal sessions.

Annual reviews and performance evaluations are the best venue to provide detailed, constructive feedback. However, if you give feedback sporadically, it won't necessarily move the needle. You must provide continuous input. Your company can likely offer assistance in the process. Companies have a myriad of tools to assist in addressing development areas. These include mid-year and year-end reviews, 360-degree feedback, and succession planning. Leverage some or all of these tools as part of an integrated development plan. If you provide feedback to your team members at key points of the year, there won't be any surprises during the year-end review.

Feedback should initially be given as close as possible to the time you notice a problem. You can deliver this feedback using meetings, conversations, or written communications. Give feedback discreetly and not in a public setting—neither in front of others nor where they can hear. Discretion will allow the person receiving the feedback to listen rather than wanting to run out of the room.

There will be times when feedback cannot wait and must be given immediately. Although these instances can be uncomfortable, highlight specific things you observed. This sends a message that you will not tolerate conduct incongruent with the company's values. Conversely, when you observe progress in a person's development goals, acknowledge and celebrate the wins. People will appreciate the recognition, whether it comes in the form of a higher year-end performance rating or public acknowledgment. This will demonstrate your commitment to work with others in a collaborative manner.

When it comes to feedback, your role in helping others cannot be sidestepped or outsourced.

"We all need people who will give us feedback. That's how we improve."

—*Bill Gates*

&

Chapter 21

IF YOU DON'T LIKE THE DIRECTION YOU'RE HEADED, CHOOSE A NEW PATH.

"One meets his destiny often in the road he takes to avoid it."

—*John de La Fontaine*

WE TEND TO take the path of least resistance. We play it safe; worried that taking a risk may end in an undesirable outcome. A rational argument can be made that we often stay on the safest path far too long. A consequence of this can be missed opportunities.

I've been a longtime admirer of serial entrepreneur Richard Branson and his story of perseverance and success. He was dyslexic and struggled through school before dropping out at the age of sixteen to start *Student* magazine. Despite this unconventional start in the business world, he proceeded to launch a succession of companies, including Virgin Records, Virgin Music, Virgin Voyages, Virgin Radio, Virgin Mobile, and Virgin Galactic. He used failures as learning experiences, and when the road he was on came to an end, he started down a new one. More often, he pursed new paths due to his interest in a new business or idea. The Virgin Group now consists of over sixty companies, spans the globe, and has tens of thousands of employees.

Colonel Sanders is another legendary example of a person who took a new road and became a household name. His father died when he was six years old and, starting at ten, he held a range of jobs that included streetcar conductor, gas attendant, and insurance salesman. In the early 1930s, he opened a restaurant featuring his fried chicken, and it grew in popularity until it closed in 1952. What many people don't realize is that Colonel Sanders was over sixty when he started down the path of what evolved into the Kentucky Fried Chicken Empire.

At sixty-two, an age when many of his peers were ready for retirement, he eagerly started this new journey to fulfill his dream. He recognized the value of creating a franchise system and began traveling the country, cooking his chicken at restaurants and signing them up as franchisees. He went on to grow the company to include over six hundred outlets and became an icon in the fast food industry. In 1964, when he was seventy-three, he sold his company to a group of investors for $2.0 million, which was a fair sum at the time.

Richard Branson and Colonel Sanders are examples of leaders who didn't take the beaten path; they carved out their own.

Changing direction is very hard, especially for those in a traditional corporate environment who have acclimated themselves to a specific culture. Despite job dissatisfaction, most people choose to stay in their roles, preferring to collect a steady paycheck rather than make a change. According to a 2017 Gallup study, 51 percent of American workers aren't engaged at work, meaning they feel no connection to their jobs. Even workers who are good at their jobs and satisfied with their leadership may have a variety of reasons for wanting to transition. Yearning for a change can come from boredom, a lack of feeling challenged, little to no connection to the company or its products, or a desire to start one's own business.

So how do you know if you're on the right path? When do you know it's time for a change?

To start, periodically assess your job satisfaction. Keep a long-term perspective in mind. It's not easy navigating through all the options. Factors to consider when leaving a company or starting your own business will vary. For example, you may be unhappy in your role but know that a new leader is coming in. It might be wise to give it some time to see if they make changes that would improve your satisfaction. Compensation or aversion to change may also influence your decision.

Any decision you make will take into account both rational and emotional factors. While no two circumstances are the same, there are some basic questions you can ask yourself: Am I satisfied in my current role? Do I have room for growth? Where do I see myself in one to five years? Am I doing this only for the money? What is my passion? Do I want to be my own boss?

Take the following job satisfaction assessment to get a general understanding of where you stand. This assessment is not meant to be a scientific evaluation, but a basic guide to gauge your overall satisfaction. Here's how it works:

1. Select ten factors and order each factor from most important to least important, with 10 being the most important and 1 the least important.

2. Rate each factor on a scale of 1–5, with 5 being most satisfied and 1 least satisfied.

3. Multiply each factor's rank by its level of importance.

4. Add up the total score.

Factors	Importance	Satisfaction	Score
Job satisfaction	10	5	50
In-job growth	9	3	27
Career growth	8	5	40
Compensation	7	4	28
Leadership	6	3	18
Work-life balance	5	3	15
Company culture	4	4	16
Skills training	3	3	9
Job security	2	4	8
Empowerment	1	2	2
Total score			213

Table 4 – Sample Job Satisfaction Assessment

You can use the factors above, substitute your own, or choose from the following list:

- Scope of role (e.g., breadth of responsibilities)

- Managing others

- Training and/or classes

- Paid college/MBA degree

- Working remote options

- Commute (distance/time)

- Amount of travel

- Time-off options (flex time, vacation, sick days, etc.)

- Giving policy (e.g., providing time off for charity work)

- Building/location amenities

Your score will range between very satisfied (237.5–275.0) and very dissatisfied (55.0–87.5).

Score	Satisfaction Level
237.5 – 275.0	Very satisfied
192.5 - 237.5	Somewhat satisfied to satisfied
127.5 - 192.5	Neither satisfied or dissatisfied
87.5 - 127.5	Somewhat dissatisfied to dissatisfied
55.0 - 87.5	Very dissatisfied

Table 5 – Job Satisfaction Assessment Scoring

A high score indicates overall happiness in your role. Conversely, a low score may indicate it's time for a change. Remember, your responses may vary over time, and any one category may be a "make or break" category. Perhaps you like your job but you don't have a good work-life balance. This could be an untenable situation and become a catalyst to seek change—even with a high satisfaction score.

Be honest with yourself and weigh your options carefully; separate out niceties from absolute necessities. If you make the decision to embark on a new journey, you must be committed to investing the time and effort required. This means research and digging into the details of the companies and roles you are considering—you don't want to be surprised because you didn't do your homework. Step up to the task; sometimes we don't know what we're capable of achieving until faced with a significant challenge. Pursuing your passion may not be easy, but it will be worth the ride.

One of the more complex decisions you'll face will be choosing between corporate positions and starting your own business.

Nine years ago I was faced with this situation, and it wasn't an easy choice to make. I'd been a "corporate guy" my whole career, but I'd always had the bug to be an entrepreneur. I was in a role that had no growth opportunities and poor work-life balance. The compensation was good, and for a time it kept me in the role. When a leadership change took place, I stuck it out for as long as I could before separating from the company. During this period, I did a lot of introspection about what I wanted to do and what would make me happy. I weighed the pros and cons between another corporate role and starting my own business.

After much wrangling between the two, I knew starting my own company was what I wanted—it was my passion. This path was filled with anxiety. Working for a corporation came with a steady paycheck, health insurance, paid vacations, etc. With a family to support and bills to pay, I wondered if I was stupid or brave to start my own firm. The key factor that tipped the scales was my desire to be my own boss. I wouldn't have to deal with office politics or be limited to specific roles. Of course, running your own business is a sink-or-swim proposition, but it was one I was willing to take. Besides, if it didn't work out, I was confident I could go back to a corporate role. I started a management consulting business, and over the course of four years, I learned a lot. I wore many hats, from sales to account management. Although I had many good clients, it was tough to manage my existing business while trying to expand my clientele. I eventually went back into a corporate role, but if I had to do it all over again, I wouldn't change a thing.

Charting a new course is not for the faint of heart. It takes fortitude, grit, and perseverance. If you a start a new venture, you will likely face skepticism and strong headwinds from more conventional minds. Whether you proactively embark on a new road or were pushed into making a change, it will be filled with twists and turns. Draw on your experience and the people in your network to assist in the transition. Your greatest asset can be a trusted advisor, mentor, or network.

It's reasonable to be hesitant to make a job change when it is shrouded by uncertainty and risk. Fear of the unknown can be paralyzing. But taking a new road, while intimidating, can open up new opportunities, increase your satisfaction, and lead to great success.

"If you create an act, you create a habit. If you create a habit, you create a character. If you create a character, you create a destiny."

—*Andre Maurois*

☙ ❧

Chapter 22

NEVER STOP LEARNING.

"The self is not something one finds. It is something one creates."

—*Thomas Szasz*

OVER THE COURSE of human history, people have had the desire to learn. You could say it's in our DNA. From the first written language, dating back over five thousand years, to the Hubble Telescope, our most astounding accomplishments have been driven by our thirst for knowledge.

It's worth looking at entrepreneurs to see just how valuable it is to make continuous learning a part of your routine. Successful entrepreneurs are exceptionally good at taking on new opportunities. Initially they may lack the knowledge or expertise for a role, but in time, they master it completely. Despite the risks, they have insatiable appetites to pursue knowledge, innovate, and build businesses.

There are several factors that give them the ability to succeed where others may fail. These include having an openness and ability to learn, seeking out expert advice, maintaining a laser-like focus on their objectives, and being resilient.

Elon Musk started SpaceX in 2002 with a vision to colonize Mars. His initial research indicated the project would be cost prohibitive, and he decided to find a better alternative. He did extensive research on existing technology and traveled across the globe to learn first-hand what was on the market. Most importantly, he *learned* by surrounding himself with engineers capable of delivering on his vision. By surrounding himself with industry specialists in rocket technology and space travel, he acquired the expertise to run his SpaceX program. Today, as proclaimed by the company's website, "SpaceX designs, manufactures, and launches advanced rockets and spacecraft." SpaceX is planning to launch the first human expedition to Mars in 2024.

Learning should be viewed as a foundational element of personal development and growth. As with professional development, you need take full responsibility for learning throughout your career. Start by creating a learning plan, and incorporate it into your broader development plan. Not everyone has a learning plan, but if you do, make sure you give it the same attention as you would give to building a competency (e.g., leadership skill).

A plan should outline what you want to learn, the learning medium you will utilize, and the outcomes you expect. It's a targeted approach to guide your growth and address gaps in your knowledge. As you build this plan, work with your leader or peers to identify the areas you should prioritize. Be proactive and flexible when it comes to your plan. As you grow, the focus of your learning will change.

There are a range of learning tools that you should consider as you build a learning plan. The possibilities span from passive learning to real-time learning, informal coaching to classroom training... even discovering new things through trial and error. Your options will vary considerably, and some will require more time and commitment than others. Companies offer a variety of training programs and often encourage their employees to take them or to attend seminars. Seeking a professional certification will require some type of classroom time and testing. Informal observation of presenters or speakers will help you shape your own presentation style. There are a lot of options to choose from, and there won't be one best way to learn; hone in on the formats that are most appropriate for you.

Learning should be enjoyable; you'll absorb and retain more if it is. Consider the time you have available and whether you have a preferred venue (e.g., classroom or online training). Trying to squeeze in classes or training sessions while working full time can be a challenge. Don't sign up if you can't commit to putting in the time needed. You will need to decide what works best for you.

Learning on the job is the most natural way to pick up new skills and knowledge. Experience is the best teacher, and you can learn from both successes and setbacks. While setbacks are hard, they're sometimes the best lessons, and they can result in a substantive change in behavior and performance. Work is a fertile learning environment where you can pick up teachings from personal experiences or through others. Observation will allow you to discern the skills, attributes, and practices you admire and want to emulate. Become a sponge and absorb as much as you can.

Align your preferred type of learning with the goals you have established. Structured classroom activity is best suited for learning new things (e.g., expanding knowledge beyond a functional discipline). Active on-the-job learning will help you develop new skills and prepare you for more senior roles. Participation in conferences or webinars is an opportunity to learn about the latest market trends or new technology being used in your industry. The more holistic an approach you can take to tapping into these sources, the better your results will be.

As you consider your career path and personal development, remember that your learning plan should be incorporated into your development plan. Learning (Chapter 22), controlling your destiny (Chapter 21), finding your passion (Chapter 10), and trusting your intuition (Chapter 2) are deeply interrelated, and each can play a role in your growth (Figure 7). Collectively, they will help you to expand your horizons, sharpen your skills, and build confidence in your abilities.

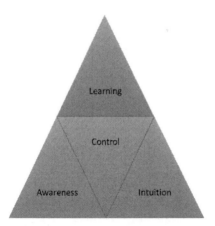

Figure 7 – Components of Growth

Your learning plan should be an integrated and comprehensive living document to guide you throughout your career. It should also be malleable, evolving as you do. As you overcome current focus areas, new ones will emerge. It is important to understand that achieving your goals doesn't mean you're done; it marks the beginning of the next chapter in your journey. This cycle will repeat itself over the course of your career. Each time around will prepare you for new challenges, increased responsibilities, and more senior roles. A learning plan will also provide you with a framework you can use to assist others on their journeys of learning and self-improvement.

"In three words, I can sum up everything I've learned about life. It goes on."

—*Robert Frost,*
as quoted by Ray Josephs

Chapter 23

SUCCESS MAY COME WITH HARD WORK, BUT DON'T DISCOUNT LUCK AND TIMING.

"Some great people are leaders and others are more lucky, in the right place at the right time. I'd put myself in the latter category."

—Steve Wozniak

ALTHOUGH HARD WORK and a personal brand are critical to success, think of them as foundational elements. Table stakes. The wild cards of luck and timing can suddenly catapult you into the fast track of success. We've all heard the saying "I was at the right place at the right time." I can tell you it's true—and these seemingly random acts of luck or timing often happen when a person least expects them. While luck and timing are not something you can seek out or buy, building your network is a concerted investment in your career that can result in long-term benefits. Your network is your ace in the hole.

The equation below illustrates how, where, and when careers can take off. There is no single route to success. Without hard work, it's difficult to be successful. Likewise, building a personal brand is a way to build credibility and improve your chances of success. These two variables are your foundation—the things you can fully control—and they will directly affect others' opinions of you, which is why their sum is multiplied by network. Network can be the single most powerful component of success—who you know can change your career in a far more lasting way than any other factor. Luck and timing, albeit more elusive factors, are raised to the nth power because although random, they can have an exponential impact on your success.

$$\text{SUCCESS} = (\text{HARD WORK} + \text{PERSONAL BRAND}) * \text{NETWORK} + (\text{LUCK} + \text{TIMING})^N$$

Although there are a variety of roads to success, the vast majority of us would surmise without hesitation that hard work is the best path to take. After all, we're taught that success comes from putting our noses to the grindstone and working long hours. It may come as a surprise that this kind of commitment isn't always enough to advance.

A senior human resource leader once asked me what percentage of success at our company I thought correlated with getting results. I thought about it and replied at least 75 to 80 percent. She said it was maybe 10 percent. The other 90 percent, she said, came from how you marketed yourself.

I remember being somewhat despondent. I placed my bets on achieving results, not on self-promotion. I couldn't believe building a personal brand far outweighed attaining results... but I was wrong. The lesson I took away from this conversation was that driving results should be treated as a foundation, not an end point. Building a personal brand was a differentiator. Although it was extremely important in that company, this may not hold true for all companies. Still, it is worth thinking about what your personal brand is and how you convey it to others.

Many successful people have a clear definition of who they are and are very good at building a personal brand around that. It's up to you to develop and hone a personal brand that conveys that you have the confidence, skills, and ability to drive change. This could mean many things. Perhaps you can be counted on to achieve tasks on time and on budget. Or perhaps you have the vision to take something to the next level.

When you begin to think about defining your personal brand, use the technique of framing the narrative. Start by brainstorming your brand goals, strengths, and career aspirations. Define your goals for both the short term and long term, know what your priorities are, ensure that you can measure your progress, and map out the path to get where you want to go. Once you have a good sense of all this, frame your story: what you want others to know about you and what you hope to achieve. Much like a company's mission statement, this should be a clear and concise statement about who you are and the reputation you want to convey. Your brand should differentiate you from others and should be coherent, realistic, and consistent.

It will take time to develop and perfect your personal brand, and initially you may find it intimidating. Some people subscribe to a philosophy of "You are who you say you are." Meaning, be persistent in presenting the brand you wish to convey, and in time, you'll have the reputation you desire.

As you build your brand, remember to make it a point to help others and foster teamwork. Everyone around you, regardless of level, should be a supporter. Don't underestimate or discount the impact of any one person's opinion and influence on decision makers.

The importance of marketing yourself shouldn't dissuade you from investing the time and effort to consistently meet or exceed expectations. In fact, that should be the cornerstone of your personal brand. But don't fall into the trap of thinking that your efforts are all you need. Hard work may not pay off in terms of promotions, raises, and bonuses. As discussed in earlier chapters, success can be elusive if it is dependent on others who are not enthusiastic in supporting you or your priorities. Timing also comes into play. You may also find yourself in the right place at the wrong time or, worse, the wrong place at the wrong time.

Although it may feel like a lesson in futility to align timing with your career aspirations, there are things you can do to increase your odds. Look for a position that is a key role, where you will have a direct impact on the business's goals. Selecting the right role today can provide you with a stepping-stone when the next promotion becomes available.

It's common for people to pursue roles that are better paying or at a higher level while not understanding how this fits into a long-term plan. Big raises are fantastic, and people are often ecstatic when they get that first paycheck, but their enthusiasm quickly erodes if they've chosen the wrong role. There are times when a lateral move will create far more opportunity over the long run in terms of compensation, level, and (most importantly) job satisfaction.

Attempting to time the next promotion is difficult. Pushing too hard or taking on a role too soon can backfire. You need to align your skills and experience to a role you desire that would be a good fit. Increase your odds by selecting a role you can excel at, in which you're likely to get noticed by management. You can also reduce the odds of having your plan backfire by working closely with your leader or a mentor. Collaborate with them to map out a plan that balances your ambition and skills. Ambition is not a bad word, but blind ambition can easily derail you. Being prepared for advancement will increase your likelihood of success when the time is right.

Timing is an elusive factor; change is constant and, more importantly, unpredictable. Our world is infused with rapidly evolving data capabilities and technology platforms, and it is easy to fall behind. Successful people have a good sense of the trends that will create substantive change. They focus on moving quickly to implement them, creating a competitive advantage by embracing the next big thing. Examples abound of how disruptors like Amazon and AirBnB have created or revolutionized their industries. Knowing when the time is right to jump on an emerging trend takes a bit of science and a bit of luck; start too soon and you run the risk of flaming out, but get the timing right and your career can take off.

Before you jump on the bandwagon of a trend, you need to understand it. Is it a fad or will it have a long-lasting impact on what you do or what your company does? Learn how important the trend is to your customers. Would they be willing to pay for this new feature or service? If you choose to wait for a competitor to move first so you can observe the results, know what success metrics they would need to attain to trigger action on your part.

Luck is a close cousin of timing and is far more capricious, but it can be exceptionally rewarding. Luck can find you by happenstance, regardless of planning or skill. An unexpected departure can open the door to a new role. Reorganization of a department can provide you with more responsibilities. A current or former leader can get a promotion and bring you with them. A chance encounter can lead to a new opportunity.

Some business leaders believe you make your own luck. For example, you can affiliate yourself with the right leader(s), company, or team. You can become an indispensable member of your team and build a reputation as a person who can get things done. Don't incessantly chase luck; chances are you won't find it. But if it finds you, congratulations are in order.

Networking is arguably the single most important component of the success equation— even more influential than luck or timing. And this one, you can control and should invest the time to cultivate. Creating strong relationships and advocacy with colleagues will set the stage for them to tap you for new opportunities.

The good news is that it is very easy to manage and cultivate your network through the use of social media sites, especially professional sites. LinkedIn is the most widely used business networking site and a great way to connect with others. You can join LinkedIn Groups with members who share your interests. There are also a multitude of specialty sites for professionals, like the CDO Summit, which brings together chief digital officers through online content and conferences. You can expand your network by writing articles or blogs and sharing what others are writing about. Treat networking as a priority. The more time you invest in it, the more valuable it will become. In time, you'll develop a strong network and a growing number of supporters.

In addition, networking provides a great opportunity to keep the door open for advancement. Remember the importance of being a passive job seeker. Networking can be one of your most important sources for career opportunities.

Hard work, luck, timing, and network are the primary factors that drive success, but they are not an exclusive list. Foresight, persistence, and passion can also contribute to your success. And you have more control over these attributes than you do over luck. One way to increase the probability of success is living the Wayne Gretzky metaphor. Wayne Gretzky has quoted his father as saying, "Go to where the puck is going, not where it has been." I've found this metaphor a very helpful reminder in my career. Focusing on where things are headed is far more important than focusing on where they've been.

You can also improve your odds of success by finding work that you're passionate about—work that inspires you; after all, love what you do and you won't call it work. Many people I've met aren't passionate about their jobs. They certainly aren't skipping and humming on their way to work, although they might be on their commute home. Compensation doesn't equate to happiness.

Granted, it can be difficult to take a role you're passionate about if the compensation doesn't meet your expectations. However, if you are truly motivated by what you do, compensation will likely take care of itself over time. In addition to cash compensation, having a job you love pays off in real and tangible ways. You're likely to be a much happier person, have a greater sense of purpose, and build stronger bonds at work and in your personal life.

One of the best books on success I've read is *Outliers* by Malcolm Gladwell, and if you haven't read it, I highly recommend you do so. Gladwell does extensive analysis on what common attributes make an individual or group great. He concludes that one common factor boils down to ten thousand hours of working diligently at a skill or trade. The people he examined were passionate about what they did and sacrificed many other aspects of their lives in pursuit of their passions. A notable example he gave was the Beatles, whose grueling schedules in the clubs of Germany transformed them from a cover band into one of the world's most prolific bands. Passion and commitment often lead to success. Remember, it's not how you start; it's how you finish that matters.

Success is the result of many factors. Some of them you have complete control over, and others you don't. Working diligently is your foundation. Building a personal brand will have a positive influence on how coworkers view you. The most important investment you should make is in developing a strong network—it is the single largest opportunity to turbocharge your career. Timing and luck will be the wildcards in your career; if you're fortunate, they'll find you when you least expect it. Keep in mind that luck is a faithless friend. It can take you to new heights or turn you into roadkill just as quickly.

Although you can't control luck or timing, there are things you can do to position yourself to take advantage of opportunities. Keep up on trends and understand where the puck is going. Many successful people were able to capitalize on their ability to place bets on the next big thing. Sometimes success comes from meticulous planning, and other times it comes because you were in the right place at the right time.

"Better an ounce of luck than a pound of gold."
—*Yiddish Proverb*

❧ ❧

Chapter 24

STRIVE TO MAINTAIN A WORK-LIFE BALANCE.

"When I was five years old, my mother always told me that happiness was the key to life. When I went to school, they asked me what I wanted to be when I grew up. I wrote down 'happy.' They told me I didn't understand the assignment, and I told them they didn't understand life."

—*Anonymous*

FAR TOO MANY people put work ahead of every other aspect of their lives. Some delay getting married or having children for the sake of advancing their careers. Others neglect their physical fitness or mental health in pursuit of the next promotion. Even if you are among the lucky few for whom your work is your passion, be sure to balance it with the other aspects of your life.

To keep things in perspective, ask yourself: When I look back at my life, what are the moments that will have the most meaning? Will it be going to staff meetings, listening to endless diatribes on work goals, attending team-building exercises, giving performance reviews, or going to town hall meetings? I'm guessing the answer is "Absolutely not."

Life is about balance.

For most of us, our personal interactions—family gatherings, vacations, spending time with friends, playing in a band, etc.—are what give meaning to life. Unfortunately, sometimes we lose sight of what's important and get lost in our work. I've witnessed people who identify themselves with their job or position sacrificing their lives outside the office.

It's easy to do. The pace of our corporate lives continues to become more hectic, and technology has enabled our jobs to encroach on our personal time. Working remotely, email, and texting often tether us to our jobs 24/7; we are always a click or an email away from work.

I worked in Manhattan most of my career, and I remember days I'd get on the train and for the next sixty to eighty minutes, I'd feverishly try to catch up on that day's emails. When I got home, my laptop was always in reach, and my mobile phone went everywhere I did. The temptation to look at my email was overwhelming and habitual. Working remotely, I now have a much better work-life balance, despite the fact that technology makes it all too easy to be online 24/7.

In extreme cases, a job can consume a person. They can't break away from work when at home or with friends. I once had a leader tell me rather sheepishly that he would go to his children's school games and bring work to do while there. Sure, there are times we need to jump on a call or work during a weekend or holiday, but this should be the exception, not the rule.

While we can't entirely separate our work and personal lives, we can balance the two. I've noticed a divergence in leadership styles as people take on greater and greater responsibility. Some people start to believe that they are infallible. They lose the perspective that their success was due to many factors: mentors, peers, and team members among them. They acquire an artificial sense of self-importance, which leads to an inflated ego. They become self-absorbed and expect others to work harder and longer in pursuit of success—and most things don't seem good enough. This attitude often lowers the motivation and morale of those who work for them.

The second group takes a different perspective. These leaders recognize that their success was due to many factors, including the support and guidance of others. They understand it takes a village, and they respect their coworkers. They encourage those under their management to work hard but not lose sight of what's most important in life. They lead by example, and members of their teams not only feel valued, but are also more energized. In fact, team members will put in more effort and be more motivated working for this type of leader.

One of my best leaders challenged me every day I came to work, and she opened new opportunities for me. This same leader would also berate me if I was working and missing a family event. She once said, "The work will still be here tomorrow. Go home and enjoy your child's game." Not only did I appreciate her guidance; I came to work the next day ready to give 110 percent. I took this leader's advice and in turn passed it on to people who worked for me. Showing compassion creates a culture that is caring and supportive, and it earns the respect of others. It will motivate them to succeed.

I know this chapter will evoke different emotions based on whether or not you subscribe to this philosophy. I've worked with people who have defined who they are based on their positions or careers. Some of these people are so committed to making their job a 24/7 undertaking that they frown on others who choose to have a work-life balance. Conversely, some of those who enjoy more balance in their lives shake their heads at those who choose long hours and make work their first priority.

I personally believe that life is much bigger than any job, and sacrificing my personal life would be a decision I'd truly regret. In the end, though, it's really up to you to choose which path you'll take—but be respectful of others who choose to take a different path.

I'd like to share an article that I wrote on LinkedIn a few years back. (I've updated it with a few minor edits to correct grammar.) I take great pride in this story, and although it happened many years ago, I still consider it a great event in my life.

THE ACCOMPLISHMENT NOT ON MY RESUME

Francis Bacon said, "In charity there is no excess." We all know that resumes are an opportunity to share an individual's skills, experience, and achievements. What resumes usually omit are some very personal yet important moments that bring meaning and a personal sense of accomplishment to our lives. In my case, it involved a Little League baseball game, and "the big moment" was a single play by an unlikely player on a team I coached. While I've had my share of milestones and tangible career achievements, there are only a handful that have given me as much personal satisfaction as this did. It came from helping a young baseball player achieve what most other kids his age could easily do on a baseball field. I'll save what he did for later in the story.

It was a typical start, as with most other Little League seasons in our town; managers select their teams in the early spring through a draft and then select their coaches. This season was not different for me—I had been a coach and was asked by the manager to help with his team. I loved coaching, so naturally I said yes. This was a recreational league and the mix of players' talents ranged from a low skill level to travel ball level. Travel baseball is for those players that excel at playing and play on a travel team in addition to their rec team. This team consisted of 11–12-year-olds, and at this age, managers and coaches focus on building and improving each player's fielding and hitting skills. Although it was a rec team and had an instructional focus, there was always friendly competition among the coaches and kids to win the championship for their age group.

At our first meeting, the manager, coaches, and kids got together to introduce everyone, and the manager announced his coaching staff. The manager and coaches also discussed the importance of coming to practices, working on fielding and hitting, and teamwork. The beginning of each season brought excitement and enthusiasm to have fun, learn, and win games. We also taught the kids about sportsmanship, working hard, and doing your best regardless of winning or losing. We always encouraged the kids to give it 100%, to have fun, and to help the team. As with every team, our players had a mix of skill levels and experience; it was up to the coaches to work with them at practices throughout the season.

The practices started to get in full swing, and we assessed each player for the positions each of them could (or wanted to) play. It is normal that all players get an opportunity to play each position unless they aren't comfortable with a particular one. Since they are young and developing their baseball skills, playing all positions gives them a chance to see what they like and where they may have the greatest aptitude. It became evident during this time that aside from the normal distribution of skill levels, we had one player who was at the very low end of the spectrum. He had trouble fielding grounders, catching fly balls, running at a normal speed—and we knew he'd have trouble keeping up with the other players. "Jimmy," it turned out, had survived a very serious illness, and as a result his body was weak, but he had a great attitude and loved to be on the baseball field.

Jimmy needed help in hitting and fielding. He wasn't very fast but knew the rules of the game and had a great attitude. Although we wanted each player on the team to play all positions, it was harder to do in Jimmy's case. He couldn't pitch as he couldn't easily reach the plate, and some positions could be quite challenging to play. Some of the stronger kids could hit the ball fairly hard, so it could be dangerous to play a position like third base where line drives came in very fast and there wasn't much time to react. We had Jimmy play several positions, and he struggled with chasing down a ball in the outfield or being able to throw the ball to a fellow player. He also had difficulty hitting a ball—some pitchers could throw fast, and it was difficult for him to make contact. He struck out many times, often looking (i.e., not swinging the baseball bat). Although he hadn't had a hit, Jimmy would enthusiastically get up to bat and try his best every time. The coaches worked with him and we got him to swing the bat, although he was often behind the pitch. But it was progress nevertheless.

During one game Jimmy got up to bat and the first pitch was a strike, but on the next pitch Jimmy swung and made contact with the ball. He got under the ball so it was a pop-up—I was the first-base coach and watched as the ball headed toward the first baseman. It was as if everything went into slow motion, and the baseball seemed as if it would never come down. I watched as the first baseman looked up and started to back up to get under the ball. In what seemed like an eternity, the ball managed to drop a few feet behind the first basemen, landing on the edge of the outfield grass. As soon as the ball landed, I turned toward Jimmy and screamed probably as loud as I could to him to run as fast as he could. Jimmy wasn't fast, and I wasn't sure if he would make it down the first base line in time, but he got to first base and got his first hit of the season. When he reached first base, I gave him a high five and I looked over to our team's dugout and all the kids were jumping up and down, yelling like we'd just won the championship game. It was great to see them support their teammate. The smile on Jimmy's face was worth a million dollars. It remains a memorable moment and one that I will never forget.

I hope everyone can experience a moment like that.

Make a conscious effort to strike a balance in your life; you can get your job done within an appropriate number of hours each week. If for some reason your job requires you to work an excessive amount of time on a regular basis, it's up to you to decide if it's worth the effort. Always test yourself with questions such as, "Am I satisfied with my work-life balance?" "Can I get my job done in a reasonable time or will long hours become the standard?" "Am I missing events or occasions that I will regret missing someday?"

Keep these questions front and center. If you don't, you'll run the risk of missing those occasions that mean the most to you.

"Imagine life as a game in which you are juggling some five balls in the air. You name them—work, family, health, friends and spirit—and you're keeping all of these in the air. You will soon understand that work is a rubber ball. If you drop it, it will bounce back. But the other four balls—family, health, friends and spirit—are made of glass. If you drop one of these, they will be irrevocably scuffed, marked, nicked, damaged or even shattered. They will never be the same. You must understand that and strive for balance in your life."

—Brian Dyson

Chapter 25

YOUR CAREER IS A JOURNEY; LAUGH, HAVE FUN, AND BE TRUE TO YOURSELF.

"A journey of a thousand miles begins with one step."
—*Lao Tzu*

LIFE IS A journey in which we have ups and downs, wins and losses, happiness and despair. I was at a Bruce Springsteen concert, and I remember him saying, "The older you get, the more it means." It is true that you have a deeper appreciation of things later in life. As we grow older and learn from life's experiences, we tend to become more philosophical about our accomplishments and regrets.

Although you can't go back and rewrite your past or change the choices you made, you can take some calculated steps to make the right choices going forward. Just as hikers prepare for a trek by wearing suitable outerwear, carrying the necessary provisions, bringing the appropriate tools, and mapping their routes, you need to gear up for your career journey. Create a well-thought-out development plan, have a clear sense of what motivates you, and find a mentor or trusted advisor. Rely on continuous self-improvement, education, training, mentoring, and learning—both from your successes and your failures.

Once you have the right equipment and gear for your journey, it's time to begin the trek. The tools you bring along will be invaluable when your path is blocked or impassable and you need to reroute. Experience will play the role of your Sherpa, guiding you along the trail. It will also reinforce things you know and teach you many new lessons.

One area that most of us don't place much importance on is having fun and laughing at work. Even if you believe it's unprofessional or inappropriate in the workplace—and maybe that's true at your company—don't underestimate the power of laughter.

Studies show a wide range of benefits of laughter across physical and mental health, as well as social relationships. One study noted how shared laughter among couples was a useful marker of healthier relationships.[5] Other research indicates a link between humor and a healthy mind and body. Correlations have been observed in areas

---

5   Kurtz, Laura E., and Sarah B. Algoe. "Putting Laughter in Context: Shared Laughter as Behavioral Indicator of Relationship Well-Being." *Personal Relationships* 22, no. 4 (December 2015): 573-590, https://doi.org/10.1111/pere.12095.

including heart disease, asthma, COPD, diabetes, rheumatoid arthritis, and skin allergies.[6]

The old adage "Laughter is the best medicine" may sound like an overused cliché, but it turns out to be true. Laughter can break the tension in a meeting, lower the defensiveness of others, and be an endearing quality. The lists in Table 6 (from the article "Laughter is the Best Medicine" on HelpGuide.org) show just how diverse and wide-ranging the benefits of laughter can be.

Physical health benefits	Mental health benefits	Social benefits
• Boosts immunity • Lowers stress hormones • Decreases pain • Relaxes your muscles • Prevents heart disease	• Adds joy and zest to life • Eases anxiety and tension • Relieves stress • Improves mood • Strengthens resilience	• Strengthens relationships • Attracts others to us • Enhances teamwork • Helps defuse conflict • Promotes group bonding

Table 6 – Benefits of Laughter

Laughter is a powerful tool. It reduces stress and tension, contributes to better teamwork and stronger relationships, and can provide long-term health benefits.

---

6   McGhee, Paul. *Humor: The Lighter Path to Resilience and Health.* Bloomington: AuthorHouse, 2010.

There is no doubt that being able to have fun and laugh is far better than the alternative. Nonetheless, be aware of your environment; there are times when work gets intense and humor could be viewed as a distraction or a sign of immaturity. Work hard, but don't dismiss the upside to having fun and laughing. Going through thirty-plus years of work absent of laughter would be unfortunate and sad.

As desirable as it is to believe we are in control of our destinies, this is a partial truth; external factors also have an impact. You can't obsess about every aspect of your career. The best strategy is to continually navigate toward your destination. Don't take your focus off your target, irrespective of what happens or how you decide to move forward. Confidence and motivation will empower you, making you more adept at circumventing roadblocks or charting alternative courses as time goes on.

If you are one of the lucky ones among us and find a job that you absolutely love, congratulations. The rest of us need to make the best of the cards we're dealt.

Whether you're first embarking on your career or well into it, remember that careers are fluid; where you end up may surprise you. Embrace the reality that spontaneity will play a part in your journey, and be adaptable as life takes you on new and unanticipated roads. This has never been more important than in today's business culture, where the speed and magnitude of change has reached dizzying heights.

No one is clairvoyant, and trying to predict precisely what will happen in your career would be a lesson in futility. The only plan you should undertake is one of preparation, with the knowledge that gaining experience will help you to deal with whatever comes your way.

And a final thought: Always remember to keep the balance in your life; don't lose sight of what's truly important.

"God gave us the gift of life; it is up to us to give ourselves the gift of living well."

—Voltaire

ॐ ॐ

Chapter 26

CONCLUSION

"If we could change ourselves, the tendencies in the world would also change."

—*Mahatma Gandhi*

WITHIN THIS BOOK are twenty-five pieces of advice that I consider to be among the best choices for my younger self. It's not designed to be the definitive list for every person; circumstances and skills vary widely among us. You may find some of these chapters pertinent today, while others may be more relevant to you in the future. Your skills will evolve as you grow, and the areas you need to focus on will change. Still, much of this advice is universally applicable, whether you're starting your career or already well on your journey.

As I look back on different situations, I cringe when I think how I handled some of them. Hindsight truly is 20/20. I've had the good fortune to have excellent leaders and get good guidance, and I've developed and honed my skills over time. Still, had I known some things sooner, the road forward would have been smoother.

I've created a list of themes you can use as a guide throughout your career. This acronym, **EMBARK**, represents six principles that can guide you on the path ahead. They are:

E – **Embrace the spirit of discovery.** Don't fear trying new things, learning, or challenging the status quo.

M – **Make it fun.** Work doesn't need to be a draining and uninspiring experience. Learn to laugh, and enjoy the people around you.

B – **Be bold.** Trust your instinct and gut, be persistent, and don't let others define who you are or what you're capable of doing.

A – **Accept that shit happens.** How you respond to change will say much about your character. Be flexible and nimble when change comes your way.

R – **Risk-taking is acceptable.** If you understand the consequences or possible outcomes, you can make decisions with more clarity.

K – **Keep the faith.** People and circumstances will throw everything they have at you throughout your career (and life). Work hard, be diligent, bring others with you, and the pieces will fall into place.

Careers are built on an evolution of skills and competencies, so don't be too tough on yourself. You're human, and there will be occasions when you make a mistake or come up short of an objective. How you deal with those occasions will speak volumes about your character.

As you transition to more senior roles, you'll go from being the net beneficiary of advice and guidance to the net provider of guidance for others. Be mindful that what was good for you as a receiver of advice should not change when it's your turn to be the provider. In simpler terms, don't be a hypocrite.

Your journey will be exciting, unpredictable, and rewarding, but be patient: the road ahead will take perseverance and faith. Be a sponge; listen, observe, test, and learn. Have the confidence to stay the course even when the dark clouds are swirling all around you and you're being pushed back by strong headwinds. That's precisely the time when you should hunker down, hold your ground, and continue to move toward your objective. Build your skills, make learning a priority, and seek out others to participate in your growth.

Enjoy the journey. I wish you luck and success.

"All of us, at certain moments of our lives, need to take advice and to receive help from other people."
—*Alexis Carrel*

ADVICE TO MY YOUNGER SELF

1. Don't let anyone else define who you are.

2. Be brave and trust your intuition.

3. Listen attentively before speaking; listen with the intent to understand.

4. Ensure you have the facts before taking action.

5. Accept change; it is the one constant that will always exist.

6. Doors will close unexpectedly, but even more doors will open.

7. Control what you can, and don't obsess over what you can't.

8. Know the risks in being dependent on others to achieve your objectives.

9. Perfectionism can be a curse; learn when good is enough.

10. Follow your passion.

11. Always embrace the spirit of discovery and innovation.

12. Find your advocates; they will support you and bring you with them.

13. Make it a priority to mentor and become an advocate for others.

14. Beware of the detractors in your career.

15. A leader's actions and words need to be completely aligned.

16. Emulate the leaders you most admire and respect.

17. If your leader doesn't support your development, assess your options.

18. Get it in writing or assume it won't happen.

19. Invest in yourself; you are accountable for your development.

20. Being candid is important, especially when giving constructive feedback.

21. If you don't like the direction you're headed, choose a new path.

22. Never stop learning.

23. Success may come with hard work, but don't discount luck and timing.

24. Strive to maintain a work-life balance.

25. Your career is a journey; laugh, have fun, and be true to yourself.

"Not all those who wander are lost."

—*J. R. R. Tolkien*

Acknowledgements

I dedicate this book to my family, friends, and coworkers who gave me the insights, lessons, and candid feedback that shaped me into the person I am today. Thank you to the many great leaders, peers, and others whom I was fortunate to work with and who generously invested their time and efforts in support of my development. Your inspiration lives on through the lessons you taught me. This book is in some ways your legacy, and I am proud to pass on the wisdom you helped to teach me so that others can also benefit from it.

Thanks also to Helene Lerner, who encouraged me to write a book to tell my story even when I didn't think I had a story to share. You were correct: there was a story to tell and this book is the proof. I am indebted to the many people who supported me, and I'd like to personally thank Elaine Hamann, Meghan Haley, and Jenny Hall. Their thoughts, guidance, and unabashed honesty kept the message of this book on track. Thank you to my editor Katherine Miller whose constructive feedback helped me tell my story more clearly.

To my family who puts up with my "humor" and supports me through good times and bad, thank you. You are always there for me without any preconditions. Even when you are being painfully honest, I know it's always done with sincerity and love. To my friends who know me best: you have been supportive and encouraged me to be myself. You have enriched the lives of my family and me, and we've shared many of life's ups and downs together. Life is a journey, and I couldn't think of a better group to share it with.

About the Author

Jeffrey Fleischman is an accomplished marketing and business transformation executive, board member, and volunteer. His career spans more than thirty years in financial services, banking, insurance, and consulting. He has held leadership positions at American Express, Chase Manhattan Bank, TIAA-CREF, Citi, Penn Mutual, Monster Worldwide, and Blue Panda Interactive. In these roles, he's led business growth and digital channel strategies, revenue generation, expense reengineering, and the improvement of customer-centric experiences. His areas of expertise include marketing, digital transformation, website and mobile design, customer acquisition, data analytics, corporate communications, and social media.

Teams under his leadership have been recognized with a Telly Award (for the TV documentary *Rugby Rising*); ranked 3rd in kasina's Top 5 Social Media Leaders in Asset Management; dubbed a leader in social media in the retirement industry by the Retirement Income Journal and the Executive Retirement Round Table; awarded a Mutual Fund Education Alliance STAR Award; received a Web Marketing Association WebAward for outstanding achievement in website development; and garnered an iNOVA Bronze Award for home page redesign.

Jeff is also a blogger and speaker. He has been a panelist at conferences including ad:tech, BRITE Conference, Social Media Week NYC, World Usability Day, and Net.Finance. In addition, he has been a guest speaker and presenter at corporate and academic meetings. Jeff has a track record of creating high-performing teams. He has been a mentor and coach for coworkers and believes helping others is an important part of being a leader.

Jeff holds a BS in finance from Syracuse University and an MBA in finance, investments and banking from Hofstra University.

Made in the USA
Columbia, SC
07 May 2019